The DITA Style Guide

Best Practices for Authors

Tony Self

Published by Scriptorium Press, the imprint of Scriptorium Publishing Services, Inc.

For information, contact:

Scriptorium Publishing Services, Inc.
PO Box 12761
Research Triangle Park, NC 27709-2761 USA
Attn: Scriptorium Press

www.scriptorium.com/books
books@scriptorium.com

ISBN: 978-0-9828118-1-8

Cover design by Alan S. Pringle and David J. Kelly

Index by Tony Self

The author developed the source files for the content in DITA. With the exception of the title page and copyright notice, page layout in this book is from Scriptorium's DITA PDF plugin processed by the Antenna House Formatter. Contact info@scriptorium.com for more information.

Contents

Introduction 7
About The DITA Style Guide 7
The role of a style guide 8
Conventions used in this book 9
Acknowledgements 9

Chapter 1: Information types and topics 11
Content models and information types 11
Information types 13
What is a topic? 18
Working with topics 21
Specialized information types 26

Chapter 2: DITA map files 29
Purpose of ditamap files 29
Topic manifest 32
Topic hierarchy 32
Relationship tables 40
Linking relationships 43
Inheritance and cascades in ditamaps 50
Embedded (or nested) ditamaps 51
DITA map vocabulary 52
The bookmap feature 59

Chapter 3: Syntax and mark-up 63
Organization of DITA elements 63
Working with mark-up 67
Element domains 73
Short descriptions 78
Lists 84
Paragraphs 91
Procedures and steps 97
Tables 108
Phrases 112
Special characters and dates 122

Chapter 4: Language and punctuation 125
- Avoiding writing for output 125
- Stem sentences, glue text, and other transitional information 125
- Punctuation in lists 128
- Titles and headings 129
- Crafting paragraphs 134
- Different languages 135
- Quotation marks 135

Chapter 5: Graphics and figures 139
- Figures and images 139
- Image file formats 141
- Image alignment, placement, and sizing 144
- Images in titles 145
- Callouts 145
- Localizing graphics 147
- Multimedia in DITA topics 147
- Figures containing tables 148
- Image maps 149
- WAI compliance 151

Chapter 6: Cross-referencing 153
- Types of cross-references 153
- The xref element 154
- Avoiding in-text cross-references to topics 155
- Cross-referencing topics and external resources 156
- Cross-referencing elements in a topic 160
- Links in related-links sections 163
- Managing cross-references 167
- Cross-references in titles 169

Chapter 7: Content re-use 171
- Content re-use definition 171
- Re-use and the DITA Maturity Model 172
- The content reference (conref) attribute 172
- Re-use practices 173
- Variables 179
- Organizing re-use topics and elements 181

Embedded topics and ditamaps 184
Advanced conref principles 184

Chapter 8: Metadata, conditional processing, and indexing 189
Conditional processing concepts 189
Condition (or select) attributes 190
Filtering and flagging 192
Other metadata 198
Indexing 203

Chapter 9: The DITA documentation process 209
Structured authoring documentation stages 209
Unit testing in a team 210
Restricting authors and limiting element choices 210
File and folder naming conventions 211
Elements for pre-publish review 215
The DITA publishing process 215
Page numbering in page layout documents 216
Content Management Systems 217

Appendix A: DITA authoring concepts 219
Introduction to DITA 219
Distinction between format and style, and data and metadata 229
Specialization 232
Generalization 233
Constraints 234

Introduction

About *The DITA Style Guide*

The DITA Style Guide: Best Practices for Authors is designed to help DITA authors implement DITA consistently by providing an authoritative reference (in the same way that *The Chicago Manual of Style* provides a reference for matters of language, writing and presentational style).

Some rules and recommendations may be controversial or contentious, and you may not agree with them. However, the purpose of *The DITA Style Guide* is to make a "ruling" one way or the other, so that at least a consistent approach can be adopted.

The DITA Style Guide is written for the DITA base content model, and not for specializations. (The nature of specialization would make it impossible to write usage rules!)

The DITA Style Guide is not an exhaustive set of rules or guidelines; it addresses the most common questions that DITA users ask, based on analysis of the *Yahoo! DITA Users Group* mailing list.

The DITA Style Guide is not authoring-tool specific, so by necessity it uses neutral code examples, rather than examples of what might appear in a *WYSIOO* editor, or other tool-specific interactions. There are many practical examples, most built around a fictitious car manual.

Style guides are often arranged alphabetically, but *The DITA Style Guide* is arranged into nine chapters covering different aspects of DITA markup. It is intended to be referenced, rather than read (it's not a "good read"), so the index is comprehensive.

The DITA Style Guide is not intended to teach you about DITA, and is aimed at people already working in a DITA environment. It assumes a working knowledge of XML principles, such as the way elements and attributes work.

The DITA Style Guide is specifically intended to be used in conjunction with, or as a supplement to, the *DITA Language Reference*, and not as an alternative to it. The online version of *The DITA Style Guide* will have links to the *DITA Language Reference.*

In the medium term, it is planned that *The DITA Style Guide* will become an open source community resource, probably in the form of a DITA-based Wiki.

The DITA Style Guide was written in DITA 1.1, and mostly follows its own recommendations! However, it's almost certain that mistakes were made, despite best efforts to eliminate them. For changes and errata, please visit http://www.ditastyle.com/.

The role of a style guide

The primary purpose of a style guide is to promote consistency. Style guides also aim to codify best practice. What the term *best practice* actually means is not universally understood or agreed. Understanding what constitutes best practice in DITA is made more challenging by the difficulty in finding agreed practices in this field, let alone best practice. Something as simple as whether paragraphs should exist within list items is not clear-cut.

A *style manual or style guide* is a set of standards governing the design and writing of documents, and usually takes the form of a printed manual. Publishing organizations, standards bodies, government agencies and publication departments within an organization are the typical originators of style manuals. Technical publication style manuals used by technical communicators, such as the *AGPS Manual of Style* and *The Chicago Manual of Style*, devote a number of chapters to the publishing process, which, in the DITA model, is removed from the technical communicator's domain. Conversely, very little space is devoted to the semantic identification of content elements, something that is core in DITA. The major purpose of a style manual is to promote consistency, and one of the difficulties of DITA adoption is working without a style guide appropriate to the DITA paradigm.

It is just as easy to lazily create poorly marked-up DITA documents as it is to create poorly styled word processing documents. To maximise the opportunities of DITA, it is important that the semantic elements are applied consistently across a publications department, and indeed across the DITA authoring community. *The DITA Style Guide* is intended to serve as an authoritative reference that defines a best practice conventions for mark-up, writing style, naming, and structure.

Conventions used in this book

Some text in this book uses special formatting:

Italics	Highlights terms and titles.
`Monospace font`	Highlights element names, attribute names, and code.

Text with a gray vertical bar indicates unequivocal rules for writing DITA content.

Acknowledgements

I would like to thank the people who helped me bring *The DITA Style Guide* project to fruition.

I owe a huge debt of gratitude to Scott Prentice, who spent a great deal of time and effort on a technical review of the content.

I give special thanks to Kris Eberlein, Gary Kilsen, Sarah O'Keefe, and Kathy Betts, who inspired, supported and/or encouraged me in this project. I "dips me lid" to John Hunt, who first got me involved in the DITA world. To the Yahoo! DITA Users Group community, and especially those such as Deb Pickett who patiently and diligently answer the questions of others, thank you!

Thank you Mike Hughes and Jen Linton for permission to reproduce some illustrations and examples in this Guide.

Thanks also to Fiona Self for undertaking the copy editing task, and to Nolwenn Kerzreho for reviewing the content. Su-Laine Yeo and the JustSystems team deserve my gratitude for their support for the project. It would also be remiss of me not to mention the help of Matthew Ellison, Suku Sinnappan, Helen Self, and Joe Welinske. To anyone whose acknowledgement I've overlooked, I sincerely apologise!

A project of this time and nature takes a lot of time and emotional energy, and I give thanks to my wife Penny Bradley for helping me every step of the way.

It is also important to me that I acknowledge the efforts of the OASIS DITA Technical Committee and the OASIS DITA Adoption Technical Committee, whose members generously donate countless hours of their considerable experience and expertise to the technical communication community.

Chapter 1: Information types and topics

What's in this chapter?

- Content models and information types
- Information types
- What is a topic?
- Working with topics
- Specialized information types

> Information is not knowledge. Knowledge is not wisdom. Wisdom is not truth.
>
> **Frank Zappa**

Content models and information types

A *content model* is an architectural framework for a collection of content, representing the structure of the data to be stored. In a structured authoring sense, a content model is a high level plan of the types of information and an appropriate structure for its storage. For example, the content model for a Frequently Asked Question (*FAQ*) of a manual might describe a hierarchy of topics, broken down into title, question, background, and answer.

When we design an information architecture for storing information (or a structure to suit our documentation), we are creating a *content (or information) model.*

Top-level elements in DITA content models are topic types (or *information types*). A typical procedure manual may include procedure, explanation, glossary and error message information types.

DITA's base content model (that is, the standard, default DITA model) defines three information types: concept, task and reference. These three types all *inherit* characteristics of a proto information type, simply named `topic`. The following diagram shows the basic information types.

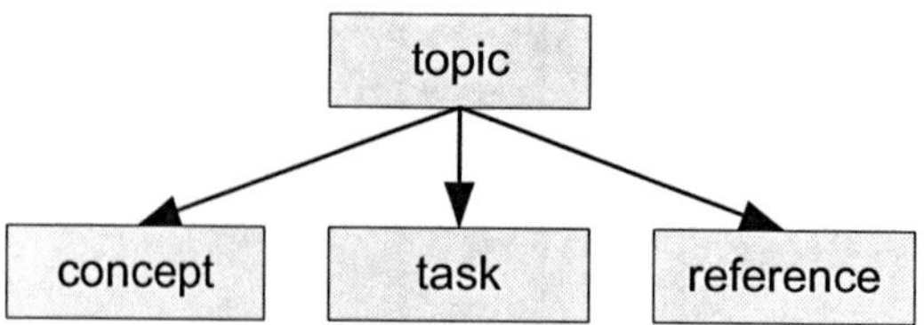

Information architects are able to specialize more types of topics, but must base their new information types on a base information type. For example, a special "error list" topic might be a specialized type of reference topic, as shown in the following diagram.

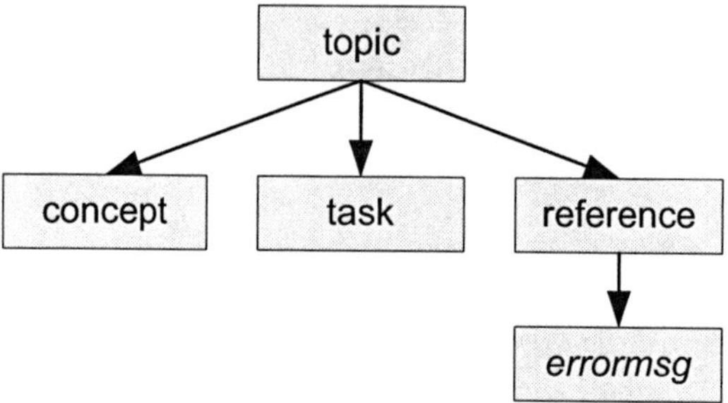

In many cases, the DITA base content model may be adequate for your needs. In other cases, your model may require the base content model to be specialized.

One method of analyzing your content model is to ask questions about your content:

- What type of topics do I need?
- Are the base information types adequate, or do I need specialized information types?
- Will I use compound topics?
- How will I associate concepts, tasks and references?
- What will my document skeleton look like?
- What single-sourcing will I do, and what metadata will I use for filtering and flagging?

Information types

The aim of all sorts of written communication is to transmit a message. The purpose, the audience and the delivery method determine the best approach.

DITA categorizes key business information by communication purpose, or *information type*. There are three base DITA information types: concept, task and reference.

The concept, task, and reference base types are sometimes called core information types, as they are considered to be universally relevant.

In DITA 1.2, the task information type was separated into *general task* and *strict task*. The *strict task* information type is the equivalent of the DITA 1.1 *task*, while the general task has much relaxed content rules.

The glossary entry (`glossentry`) information type was introduced in DITA 1.2 as a specialization of the concept information type.

> **Note:** In *The DITA Style Guide*, the term *task information type* means the *task* information type in DITA 1.0 and 1.1, and the *strict task* information type in DITA 1.2.

Concept

Concept topics are used to document conceptual or overview information. They contain background information that users must know before they can successfully work with a product or within a process. Concepts can be broken into sections, but they are primarily comprised of simple paragraphs and unordered lists.

Concept topics answer the question "what is?".

The root element of a concept topic is `concept`.

Task

Task topics are used to document the steps of a particular task or procedure, or to document the stages within a high level process. Task topics are the building blocks for task-oriented documentation. Task topics are more strictly structured than concept and reference topics.

Task topics address the question of "how to?".

The root element of a task topic is `task`.

General Task

In DITA 1.2, the task information type was separated into *general task* and *strict task*. Technically speaking, the *general task* is now the base task information type, because strict type is implemented as a *constrained* version of general task. (DITA 1.2 also introduced the constraints feature, which allows the rules of an information type to be tightened in a simpler way than otherwise creating a specialized information type.)

Figure 1: Task information types in base DITA 1.2

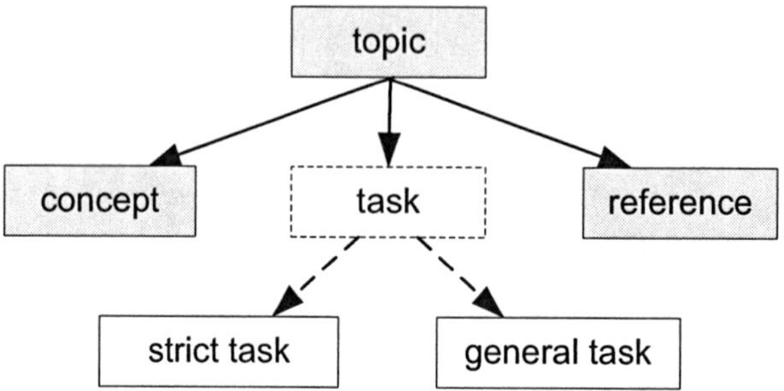

For documenting most procedures, the *strict task* is the more appropriate choice. Conceptually, it is best to think of the *task* information type as meaning *strict task*. The *strict task* information type is the equivalent of the DITA 1.1 *task*, while the general task has much more relaxed content rules.

> **Note:** In *The DITA Style Guide*, the term *task information type* means the *task* information type in DITA 1.0 and 1.1, and the *strict task* information type in DITA 1.2.

Wherever possible, you should prefer the *strict task*. If your organization's content model is more appropriately served by general task, then stick to general task across the document repository. Avoid mixing *strict task* and *general task* in the same publication.

Reference

Reference topics are used to describe features of sets of things, such as codes, types and commands. Information that normally demands tabular presentation probably belongs in reference topics. Catalogues, directories and bibliographies are good examples of reference topic information. Reference topics are often organized into tables.

Reference topics contains "facts without explanation".

The root element of a reference topic is `reference`.

Glossary entry

The *glossary entry* (`glossentry`) information type is part of the DITA standard, but is not widely seen as one of the base DITA information types. Technically, it is a specialization of the base concept information type.

Figure 2: Base and specialized information types

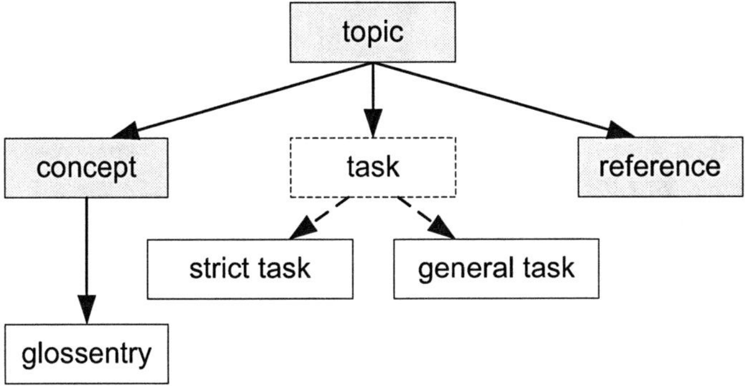

The structure of `glossentry` is quite simple. There are two main block elements: `glossterm` and `glossdef`. The `glossterm` element (a specialized `title`) contains the name of the term, while the `glossdef` element (a specialized `abstract`) contains the definition of the term.

Just one term should be defined in one glossary entry topic.

A document's glossary of terms is created by grouping glossary entry topics in the ditamap. Except for small documents, using a separate ditamap for the glossary, and then embedding the glossary ditamap in the main map for the collection, is the architecture most easy to manage.

The linking of a term occurring in-line in a normal content topic to its relevant `glossentry` definition is a matter of associating the term (semantically identified in a `term` element) with the hypertext reference (`href`) or the key reference (`keyref`) of the glossary topic.

The root element of a glossary entry topic is `glossentry`.

Composite (*ditabase*)

In the early days of DITA, the composite, or *ditabase*, information type was developed as a way of collecting topics together for publication before the *ditamap* was created.

The ditabase composite topic allows other topics (of any information type) to be nested within it.

The ditamap is a superior method for collecting topics together, and should always be used in preference to ditabase.

However, ditabase still has some use as a container for re-use information, because it allows concept, task, reference and other information type elements to be contained within the same topic. This can be useful if you want to organize snippets of conref source information into a single topic.

Do not use ditabase as a means of creating an output topic with mixed information types. If this is necessary, you should use the `chunk` attribute as an alternative.

The root element of a ditabase topic is `dita`.

Topic (proto information type)

All DITA information types have “evolved” from the *topic proto information type*. The *topic* type is *weakly information typed*, or even *untyped*, in that it has generic rather than semantic elements. It is designed as a starting point for specialization, and not for use as a container for structured, semantic content.

Apart from for specialization, the other purpose of the untyped topic information type is to store legacy information during the migration of style-based documents to DITA. For example, when migrating untyped HTML content to DITA, it can be useful to first convert HTML topics to untyped DITA topic, for later conversion to correctly typed DITA information types such as concept, task and reference.

The root element of an untyped topic is `topic`.

Identifying the information type

An important skill of an author working in a DITA environment is *typing* information correctly into information types.

Of the three base DITA information types:

- *Concept* topics are used for overviews of tasks or overviews of reference information. They tend to be short and simple.
- *Task* topics contain procedural steps.
- *Reference* topics detail properties and other reference (as opposed to narrative) information, typically in tabular form.

In some types of documents, an instruction may be described with a set of concept, task and reference topics. For example, the use of a car's alarm system may be covered by:

- "Alarm systems" (concept)
- "Setting the alarm" (task)
- "Alarm codes" (reference)

Such a set of topics would be associated using a *reltable*, so that the topics would be linked or associated in the deliverable document. A typical procedure will require a concept topic and a task topic, and may require a reference topic.

While task information is generally easy to identify, it can be difficult to distinguish concept from reference information. Table 1: Characteristics of concept and reference topics explains some of the characteristics of concept topics compared with reference topics.

Table 1: Characteristics of concept and reference topics

	Concept	**Reference**
Purpose/Function	Explanatory	Fact
Access Frequency	A few times	Repeatedly, when needed
Book Context	Front, Middle	Back

	Concept	Reference
Content or Data	Content	Data

What is a topic?

DITA is designed around a topic-based information architecture; topics are the building blocks of DITA documents. The topic-based approach in DITA is similar in many ways to the topic-based approach of most hypertext systems.

The *DITA Architectural Specification* defines a topic as follows:

> A topic is a unit of information with a title and content, short enough to be specific to a single subject or answer a single question, but long enough to make sense on its own and be authored as a unit.

The DITA approach is that the author writes a topic independently of the publication in which it may eventually be published. (A publication is created by assembling topics into a hierarchical structure and "publishing" the collection of topics to a reading format.) This *topic-oriented writing* is a disciplined approach to writing that emphasises modularity and re-use of concise units of information.

A topic is created as a standalone chunk of information, typically limited to one idea. A well-written topic will fully convey that idea in one reading. Technically, a DITA topic can be as minimal as just a title, but practically that can only occur when the title alone conveys the idea completely. A topic is stored in its own file. Topics are categorized into different *information types*.

Although topics can technically be broken down into sections, you must take care to ensure that sections are not used as an alternative to topics. Sections should only be used where the single idea being conveyed in the topic is complex. Using sections instead of topics detracts from modularity.

> **Note:** A number of DITA (source) topics can be later assembled into a single deliverable topic, such as an XHTML topic. DITA includes a `chunk` attribute for this purpose. You should not create topics in

DITA according to how you want the information chunked in the deliverable reading format.

How detailed should a topic be?

The amount of information per topic within a publication is sometimes referred to as *topic granularity*. A DITA topic should contain just one idea or answer a single question.

In some cases, a topic may be extremely short, as in the following example of an emergency procedure for a jet fighter aircraft.

```
<task>
<title>Engine failure below 10,000 feet</title>
<taskbody>
 <steps>
  <step><cmd>Eject.</cmd></step>
 </steps>
</taskbody>
</task>
```

In other cases, a topic describing a very complex procedure, a very complex concept, an extensive glossary, or a lengthy reference table, may be the equivalent of many pages long. For example, a reference topic listing all the makes and models of cars of the 20th century is very lengthy, but still covers just one subject.

A topic should be as short as possible, but long enough to be independent of other topics. In other words, it must make sense on its own in any context.

Granularity - one file per topic

Each DITA topic should be stored in its own file. Although the *ditabase* (or composite) topic type technically permits multiple topics to be nested in a single container topic file, this approach should be avoided. The smaller the topic unit, the greater the opportunity for re-use.

Although it is possible to use the `chunk` attribute to merge multiple DITA source topics into a single output topic when publishing to topic-based formats such as XHTML, the simplest approach is one source topic to one output topic.

Chunking information into topics

With topic-based documentation, the way in which information is broken down and *chunked* into topics is very important. A user guide with one very long topic organized into sections is poorly chunked. Topics should be small, self-contained, granular units of content. In general, the smaller the topic size, the greater the chance that topic can be re-used in another deliverable document.

The process of *chunking* involves analyzing the components of the information to be documented, identifying the blocks of content that can stand alone as information units, and then splitting those units into separate *chunks*.

In DITA, standalone *chunks* can be organized into topics, sections within topics, or topics within topics. You should aim to have separate topics for each chunk, and to avoid sections and composite topics.

Information in a DITA source topic doesn't have to be delivered at the same granularity. For example, a family of DITA topics may be output as a single HTML topic. (The `chunking` attribute in the `topicref` element in the ditamap is used for this purpose.)

Avoiding chunk structure in topics

A *chunk*, in this context, is an identifiable block or unit of information, and *chunking* is the process of organizing information into units.

DITA has a `section` element, used to divide topics into subsets of information directly related to the topic. When writing content in DITA, you will sometimes have to choose between chunking information into separate topics, or using a single topic with the information chunked into sections within that topic.

In nearly all cases, separate, simple topics should be preferred to sections.

One of the reasons why `section` elements should be avoided is that they result in hierarchy and sequence (document structure) being embedded in the topic. If a chunk of content is contained within a section instead of a topic, it must always appear in the same sequence within the containing topic. Structured as a topic, the information can appear in any sequence, in any hierarchy, in any collection.

Sections are more difficult to re-use; the smaller the granularity of a document, the more re-use opportunities there are.

Cases where sections may be appropriate include single topics where the idea covered has many facets. DITA does not permit sections within sections (*nested sections*).

It is technically possible to nest topics of different information types within a *ditabase* (or *composite*) topic type. However, the *ditabase* topic is not intended for this purpose. It should only be used to contain re-use elements for mixed information types.

Using separate DITA topics doesn't mean that the topics must be generated as separate topics in the output. If necessary, DITA source topics can be grouped into a single output topic, for example, through the `chunking` attribute in the ditamap `topicref`.

The ditamap is the correct place for hierarchy and sequence to be recorded.

Working with topics

Topics are the building blocks of DITA, and a methodical apporach to topic creation will result in consistent and more effective documents.

Stem topics

A *stem topic* is a short topic that contains very little content, instead providing pointers (cross-reference links) to related information. Stem topics are used as navigation aids for online documents.

Stem topics should not contain descriptions of the related topics; instead, the publishing process should be used to automatically insert links and short descriptions to the related topics. Stem topics are typically *parent* topics in a Table of Contents hierarchy, where the related topics are *children* of the (stem) parent. Avoiding content in stem topics reduces the amount of redundant writing (writing a short description twice, once in the stem topic and once in the target child topic), and avoids embedded links that reduce re-usability (as the stem topic with an embedded link can only be used if the linked topic is part of the same collection).

For example, the following stem topic is not desirable, as it includes content and embedded links.

Figure 3: Example of stem topic with embedded links and table formatting

Managed Security Services (MSS) overview

Managed Security Services customers maintain high levels of security awareness and control v experts perform day-to-day security management tasks. The Managed Services Customer Por real-time access to reports, charts, and utilities, so your staff can quickly review logs, submit p enter service requests.

The following services are available to IBM Internet Security Systems MSS customers.

Service	Description
Managed Protection Services for Networks, Servers, and Desktops	Managed Protection Services for Networks, Servers, and Deskto industry's only guaranteed protection solutions, including money performance-based Service Level Agreements (SLAs) and the in protection warranty.
Vulnerability Management Services	Vulnerability Management Services provide real-time manageme servers, firewalls, switches and other devices.
Security Event and Log Management Services	Security Event and Log Management Services enable organizati analyze, correlate, and trend security and network events, while and remediation workflow.
Managed IDS and IPS Services for Networks and Servers	Managed IDS and IPS Services for Networks and Servers preven protecting companies from attacks stemming from points inside network perimeter.
Monitored and Managed Firewall Services	Monitored and Managed Firewall Services deliver advanced, flexi based, customized expert monitoring, management and analysi detect, prevent and respond to the evolving threat spectrum.

You should instead use relationships in the ditamap to automatically generate links to the child topics, and automatically place the short descriptions of those child topics. This approach would result in the following deliverable document.

Figure 4: Example of stem topic with generated links

Managed Security Services (MSS) overview

Managed Security Services customers maintain high levels of security awareness and control while protection experts perform day-to-day security management tasks. The Managed Services Customer Portal offers secure, real-time access to reports, charts, and utilities, so you can quickly review logs, submit policy changes, and enter service requests.

The following services are available to IBM Internet Security Systems MSS customers.

> **Managed Protection Services for Networks, Servers, and Desktops**
> Managed Protection Services for Networks, Servers, and Desktops provide the industry's only guaranteed protection solutions, including money-back, guaranteed, performance-based Service Level Agreements (SLAs) and the industry's only protection warranty.
>
> **Vulnerability Management Services**
> Vulnerability Management Services provide real-time management and analysis of servers, firewalls, switches and other devices.
>
> **Security Event and Log Management Services**
> Security Event and Log Management Services enable organizations to archive, analyze, correlate, and trend security and network events, while managing response and remediation workflow.
>
> **Managed IDS and IPS Services for Networks and Servers**
> Managed IDS and IPS Services for Networks and Servers prevent downtime by protecting companies from attacks stemming from points inside and outside the network perimeter.
>
> **Monitored and Managed Firewall Services**
> Monitored and Managed Firewall Services deliver advanced, flexible, intelligence-based, customized expert monitoring, management and analysis of firewall data to detect, prevent and respond to the evolving threat spectrum.

Although it may not have the same aesthetic appeal as the manually created stem topic, the benefits of re-usability and efficiency outweigh the look-and-feel.

Disambiguation topics

Disambiguation topics help clarify ambiguity when one term or topic title may relate to a number of different topics. For example, a term "ABS" may stand for "Anti-lock Braking System" or for "Automatic Brightness Sequencer". A disambiguation topic is typically a single topic explaining the different uses of the term, and links to the relevant alternative topics.

Avoiding linking in topics

For content to be truly separated from format, structure, context and delivery, there can be no links embedded within the topic content, because links contain *context*.

Embedded links create a dependency upon the linked topics; the topic can only make sense if the target topics for each of the links it are delivered alongside it. If a target topic is not included in the same collection as the topic, then the link will be broken.

DITA includes automatic linking mechanisms based on relationships established in *relationship table (reltable)* within the ditamap. Because the ditamap defines the collection of topics to be delivered as a publication, this is a more logical place for links between topics in the collection to be defined.

The difference between processes, procedures and tasks

A process is an upper level description of a series of major steps required to accomplish an objective. Processes are generally made up of procedures or tasks. A task is another way of describing a procedure. Another way of putting it is that a process is a sequence of tasks.

DITA does not distinguish between processes and tasks, although DITA 1.2 does provide *strict task* and *general task* variants of the *task* information type.

The term *task* is used in DITA, in preference to procedure, work instruction or unit rule. A *task topic* contains one procedure or task, and is made up of a series of steps. In turn, steps are made up of commands (or actions), step results, and perhaps substeps.

In a process, each step outlines the result or outcome of a task, and that step is typically linked to the task topic that details that step at a lower level.

Using `sectiondiv` and `bodydiv` Elements

DITA 1.2 introduced `sectiondiv` and `bodydiv` elements. These elements mimic the HTML `div` element, which is used to group blocks of content that don't have any formal (or semantic) connection. In

HTML, the `div` element is mainly used in conjunction with CSS and Dynamic HTML.

The `bodydiv` element allows block elements in the body of a topic to be grouped and treated as a single unit in processing. The `sectiondiv` element likewise allows block elements in a section of a topic to be grouped and treated as a single unit. The two elements are intended as an aid for the author, and their use will be invisible to the reader of the deliverable document.

The most common use of `sectiondiv` and `bodydiv` is to group paragraphs so they can be re-used (through a *conref*) as one unit, as an alternative to *conref spanning*, where a start and end point of a conref source is specified.

As you should avoid sections (and prefer separate topics), the need to use the `sectiondiv` element will be limited.

An example of the `bodydiv` element is:

```
<conbody>
...
<bodydiv id="ebd_intro">
<p>The EBD functions by adjusting the distribution
of braking force to the
rear wheels in accordance with the vehicle's loading
condition and speed.</p>
<p>The EBD system is an integral part of the ABS
system and uses some of the
ABS system's components to perform its function of
optimizing the
distribution of braking force. If any of the ABS
components used by
the EBD function fails, the EBD system also stops
working.</p>
</bodydiv>
</conbody>
```

The two paragraphs in the example might be re-used in another topic as:

```
<conbody>
<p>Your vehicle is equipped with Electronic
Brakeforce Distribution (EBF).</p>
<bodydiv conref="c_ebd.dita#concept_ebd_explanation/
ebd_intro" />
...
</conbody>
```

Specialized information types

DITA is designed around topic specialization. Many types of content will not suit the structure of the DITA base information types of concept, task and reference, but new information types, with a structure to exactly suit the nature of the content, can be evolved from the base types.

A specialized information type is always derived from another DITA information type, so that you only need to define how your information type is different from what it is based on.

Types of specialization

There are two types of specialization:

- structural specialization (topic or map level), and
- domain specialization (element level).

Structural specialization is used to design complely new information types, such as an architecture to suit Java API documentation.

Figure 5: Examples of specialized information types

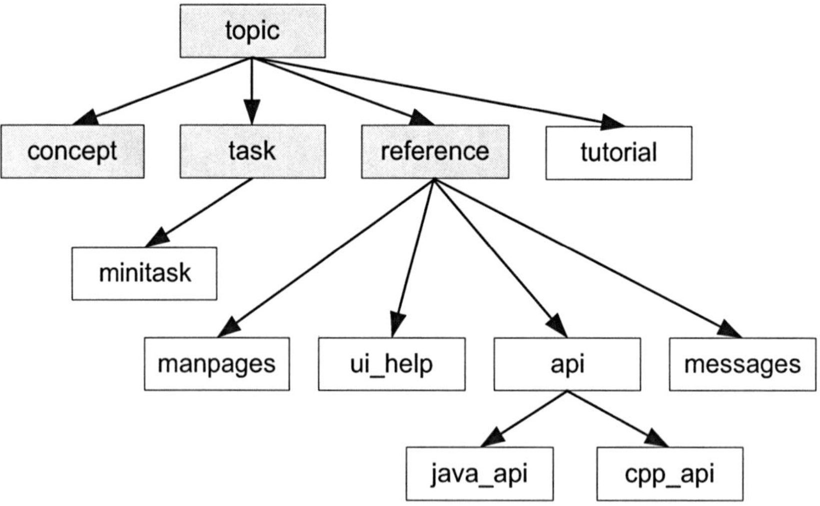

Domain specialization is used to modify the design of the semantic elements and attributes within an information type, such as creating a new element named `partnumber`.

Sometimes, *configuration* is confused with specialization. Configuration is a technique where the author or organization chooses not to use all the DITA elements and topic types. Configuration restricts, but does not extend. Specialization defines new elements and information types.

"Official" specializations

A number of sub-committees of the OASIS DITA Technical Committee have been formed to look at ways of making DITA more suitable for specific purposes. For example, the DITA Semiconductor Information Design Sub-committee is working out how to make DITA suit semiconductor documentation. The result of the sub-committee's work will most likely be semiconductor specializations. Such specializations might be viewed as being "official", in that they are published and supported by the governing DITA Technical Committee, rather than being just a company-specific specialization.

For specializations to be effective, processors have to be written to work with the specialized DITA. For example, once your DITA content uses other than base content model DITA, you can't get your document to look "special" unless you write a processor specific to your specialization.

To specialize or not to specialize

One of the most difficult questions for DITA adopters is whether or not to specialize.

One of the impediments to specialization is the perceived technical difficulty in both designing the structure and coding the necessary schema files. Certainly, specialization is beyond the skills of a typical technical writer. However, a DITA project team should include a broad range of expertise, and outsourcing tasks that are beyond the capabilities of the team is a good strategy.

On the other hand, unless you fully understand the reasons why the base content models are inadequate for your own content, you should not specialize.

Before designing your own specialized information type, you should check to ensure that there is no public domain specialization that would suit your needs. A number of public domain specializations have been developed by OASIS DITA sub-committees, industry groups, and individuals.

Limits on specialization

Specialization is not an open-slather, no-rules process. It is a formal, defined process with limitations.

The main requirements of specialization are:

- You cannot make your specialized DITA less restrictive than the DITA *base content model.*
    - You cannot make a mandatory element optional, and you cannot make a mandatory attribute optional.
    - You cannot allow elements in positions that are not allowed by the base content model.
- You cannot add new element-specific attributes. You can only create new global attributes (or attributes of elements in the base content model.

Chapter 2: DITA map files

What's in this chapter?

- Purpose of ditamap files
- Topic manifest
- Topic hierarchy
- Relationship tables
- Linking relationships
- Inheritance and cascades in ditamaps
- Embedded (or nested) ditamaps
- DITA map vocabulary
- The bookmap feature

> Hic sunt dracones (Here be dragons!)
>
> **Phrase on the 16th Century Lennox Globe map**

Purpose of ditamap files

DITA map (or *ditamap*) files have three primary purposes:

Topic Manifest To define the topics to be processed into the output publication.

Hierarchy Definition To define the sequence and hierarchy of topics in the output so that the heading levels, table of contents, parent-child links, and other navigation pathways (such as breadcrumb links) can be constructed.

Linking Relationships To define the relationships between topics so that related topics links and other context-specific links can be automatically constructed.

A map has two main components: the hierarchy (of which there is one per map), and the relationship table (of which there can be none or many). Both are primarily made of *topic references* (`topicref` elements).

A *ditamap* file is not a topic: it contains no content. It is, however, a type of DITA XML file. A *ditamap* file can also contain publication- or output-specific metadata.

You can create as many ditamaps as you need. For example, you might create one map file for your *Supara Impress XRW Owner's Manual*, another for the *Supara Impress XR Owner's Manual*, and another for the Supara Impress Web site.

Publication and collection defined

In the DITA sense, a *publication* is the name given to a set of topics that are assembled (from a pool of DITA source files) to form a deliverable document. Because the term *publication* evokes a mental image of a printed work, the terms *output* or *deliverable* are sometimes used for differentiation.

When produced as a printed document, we might call the output of the DITA publishing process a "book". When produced for online delivery, we might call the output a "Web site". When produced as a CHM file, we might call the output a "Help system".

The term *collection* is used to describe a potential publication in the DITA source. A ditamap *collection* is processed to become a *publication.* In other words, *collection* describes the source content, while *publication* describes the output format. A collection is defined in DITA through a ditamap, or multiple embedded ditamaps.

The process of transforming DITA source into an output format is known as *publishing*, *processing*, or *transformation*, and the software tools for the process are known as *processors*, *transformers*, or *publishing engines*.

Anatomy of a ditamap file

The vocabulary of a ditamap file is quite simple. The principal element is the topic reference (`topicref`), which is simply a link to a topic to be included in the collection. The `topicref` elements can be nested, allowing you to build a hierarchy of links to topics.

Other elements which you can use to refine the hierarchy are:

`topichead` an unlinked heading (or group) in the hierarchy

`topicgroup` a way of grouping `topicref` elements together without affecting the hierarchy (used for applying characteristics to a group of topics at a time)

`topicmeta` metadata for the topic that applies specifically to the context of the publication defined by the ditamap

As well as linking to topics, `topicref` elements can link to other ditamaps, thus permitting the embedding and re-use of ditamaps.

A ditamap file may also contain one or more *relationship table (or reltable)* sections. A *reltable* is made up of rows (`relrow` elements) of cells (`relcell` elements), usually with a header row (`relheader` elements). Cells contain `topicref` elements that link to topics. The relationship between `topicref` elements within rows and cells determines how generated links will appear in the output.

Generated relationship links

When a ditamap is *processed* (transformed into a reading format), particularly to a hypertext format, cross-referencing links can be automatically generated. For example, the samples following show some automatically generated related topics links.

Figure 6: Generated links in HTML output

You can save money on canned goods by:

- buying from chain or discount grocery stores
- buying larger cans

Parent topic: Shopping for groceries

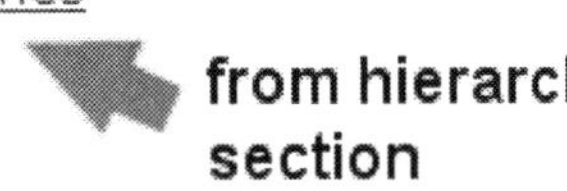

Related concepts
About produce

Related tasks
Choosing produce
Buying canned goods

from reltable section

Related reference
Available produce
Available canned goods

Figure 7: Generated links in PDF output

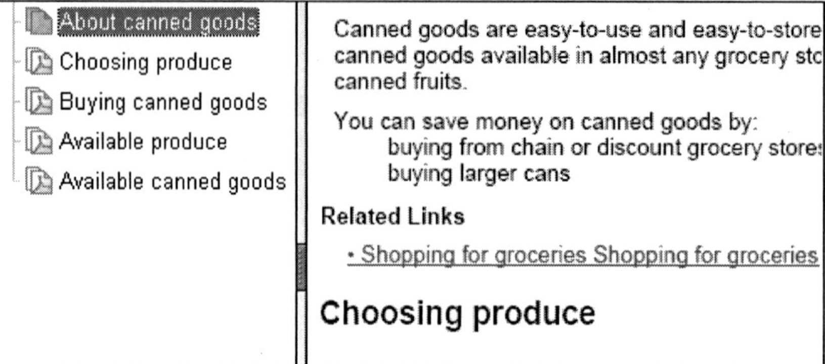

Topic manifest

Topics to be included in the output are referenced through `topicref` elements in the ditamap. The `topicref` elements (and specializations of `topicref`) are used both in the hierarchy and the relationship table sections of the map. If a ditamap includes an embedded map (a `topicref` referencing a ditamap rather than a DITA topic), then topics referenced by `topicref` elements in the embedded map will also be included in the output.

Simplistically, any topic referenced in the ditamap will be included in the output. An exception is for topics with the `topicref` element's `print` attribute set to no; these topics will not be included in page layout outputs (such as PDF).

Topic hierarchy

A topic-based document architecture relies on a device to bind the topics together into a structured output publication. A Help system is a good example of a topic-based document architecture. The binding device in Help systems is called the *Table of Contents, or TOC*. The *TOC* is used by the author to choose the topics that will be included in the publication, and the order in which they will be presented in navigation. In most Help systems, the *TOC* is also presented to the reader as an expandable and collapsible tree of links, which the reader can use to navigate through the document.

Figure 8: Example of a Table of Contents (from a Help file)

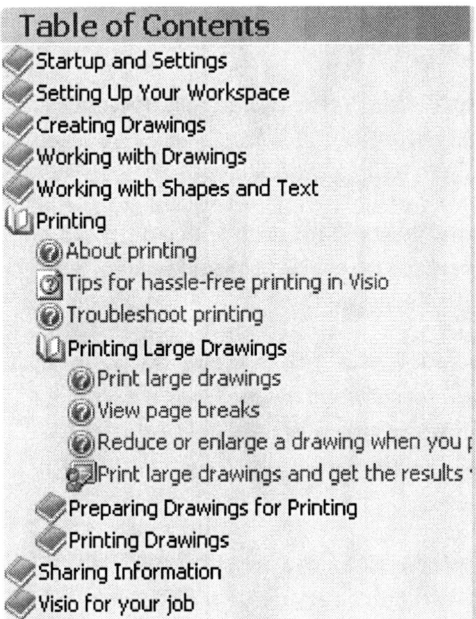

Being topic-based, DITA also needs a TOC-type device to bind *collections* of DITA topics together, and the *ditamap* is used for that purpose. The ditamap not only specifies what topics are to be included in the output, but specifies the sequence and hierarchy of the topics through nested `topicref` elements organized into a tree structure.

When DITA is transformed into a Help format, the ditamap is used to derive the appropriate *TOC* file. When DITA is transformed into a page layout format such as PDF, the ditamap is used to derive the Table of Contents and the heading styles in the output content.

Designing a topic hierarchy

Structuring the content of a document is one of the most important steps in the authoring process. It is here that you establish the logical relationship between topics, and add context to the set of topics.

Some theoretical considerations to make when deciding on the structure of topics include the following.

- The human mind can manipulate about four concepts at a time.
- Humans make better decisions when presented with groups of seven choices (Miller's Law)[1].

Translated to a document structure, this points to an ideal document structure made up of *parent topics* with seven *child topics* at every level, and no more than four *generations* of topic families.

A three level hierarchy with seven topics per menu will permit 343 pages. Four layers of ten topics permits up to 10,000 topics, which is more than enough for even the largest manuals.

The human mind thinks in associative, rather than linear, patterns. Thus we "get on the wrong track", and "forget how we got onto this subject". The human brain stores information in this way also, by finding a similar experience and associating it with the current experience ("this tastes like vinegar").

In DITA, concept information is separated from task and reference information. This makes it more difficult to structure a document purely around the goals of the reader, unless the nature of the information allows the creation of standard sets of one concept, one task and one reference topic. Such an information model would permit a TOC structure such as:

- Starting
    - Engine principles (concept)
    - Starting the engine (task)
    - Engine specifications (reference)

An alternative approach would be to group concept topics, task topics and reference topics, resulting in a high level structure such as:

- Car Concepts

[1] Miller, G. A. (1956). The magical number seven, plus or minus two: Some limits on our capacity for processing information. Psychological Review, 63(2), 81-97.

    - Starting
    - Driving
    - Stopping
- Car Tasks
    - Starting
    - Driving
    - Stopping
- Car Reference Information
    - Starting
    - Driving
    - Stopping

In reality, however, most information models do not have such a repeatable structure. More likely is that there will be a concept topic that has three or four related task topics, with a reference topic that might be associated with a dozen concepts.

The best structure for a particular document is not something that can be easily prescribed; it is the responsibility of the author to devise a logical structure that will support the aims of the deliverable document.

You should consider the following questions when designing a TOC and a structure for your topics:

- What level of detail will be used?
- How much information will each node contain?
- What nodes will connect to what other nodes?
- What sort of links will be used?
- What entry points are needed?

Two more specific guidelines to adopt are:

- Designing your structure with a single node at the top of the tree hierarchy (a "mother-of-all-topics") from which all other topics branch. This helps ensure logical *breadcrumb* links and other navigation pathways.
- Do not use topic headings (`topichead` elements). Instead, use stub or summary topics: topics that contain only a title. The publishing process can automatically build the content of such stub topics based on the short descriptions of its child topics.

Heading levels and ditamaps

In DITA, each topic is written as a standalone chunk of content. The style in which a topic title, for example, is eventually presented to the user is determined by the position of the topic in the relevant ditamap.

For example, if a topic called "About SD Cards" is located at:

```
Camera Model 700 > Storing Pictures > Memory > About
SD Cards
```

then its heading style in RTF output might be `Heading 4`.

If that same topic is re-used in a different ditamap, located at:

```
Taking Pictures > Storing > About SD Cards
```

then its heading style in RTF output might be `Heading 3`. The topic is identical, but its presentation is appropriate to the output context.

And it gets better! Topic titles can be different in different ditamaps.

Controlling the top node (default topic)

When a ditamap file is processed into a Help format, the first topic in the ditamap hierarchy becomes the first (or default) topic displayed. In some Help outputs, it also becomes the topic displayed when the **Home** button in the tri-pane navigation panel is selected.

Some Help formats allow for the nomination of a topic other than the first topic as the default page, and perhaps yet another topic as the *Home topic*. DITA currently has no facility to record such an alternative *Home topic* in the ditamap.

In Eclipse Help outputs, the *TOC* generated from the ditamap includes the `map` element as its top node. This can cause some confusion to the user, because the title highlighted in the TOC is different from the title of the displayed topic.

In the first example following, an Eclipse Help system is displaying an information set using the collection's home address. The TOC is highlighting the ditamap's `map` element title, while the topic associated with the first `topicref` in the ditamap is displayed. The second example shows the same document, open at the home address, in Microsoft HTML Help format. In this type of output, the `map` element in the ditamap is ignored when the TOC is generated.

Figure 9: Example of map title (with no associated topic) displaying in Eclipse Help TOC

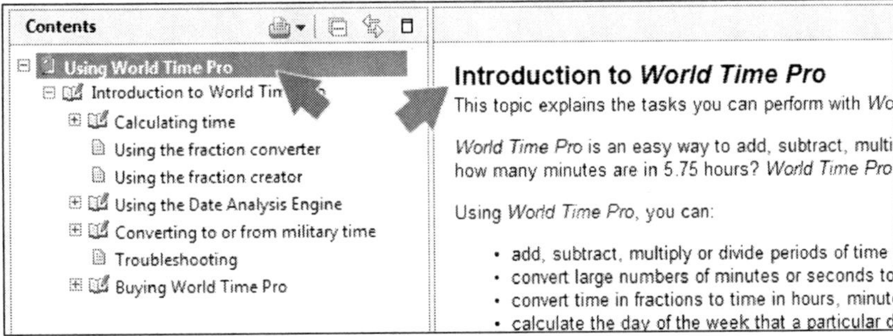

Figure 10: Example of first topic title displaying in HTML Help TOC

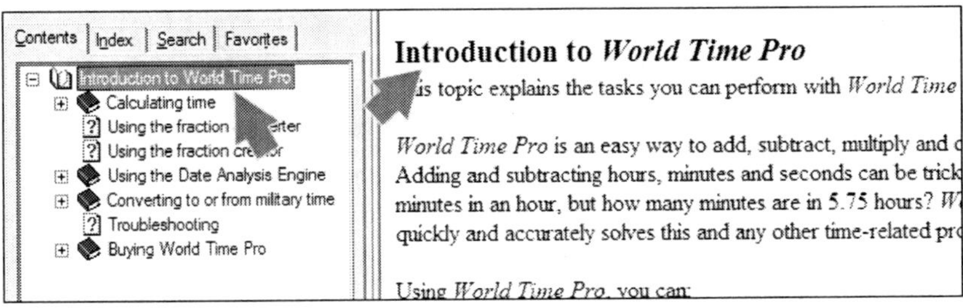

One workaround is to structure the ditamap so that the first node is a "childless" `topicref` element with its `toc` attribute set to no, and ensuring that the title of the `map` element is the same as that first topic. This will result in the first topic not appearing in the TOC, creating the illusion that the top node links to the topic. The mark-up for the map would therefore follow this pattern:

```
<map title="Introduction to World Time Pro">
  <topicref href="c_WorldTimePro.dita" toc="no"/>
  <topicref href="c_CalculatingTime.dita">
    <topicref .... />
    <topicref .... />
    ....
  </topicref>
  <topicref href="c_FractionConverter.dita" />
  ....
</map>
```

Although this workaround will deliver a good result, take care that focusing on the output format (the form) doesn't result in compromises to the information design (the content), so that the separation of content and form is honored.

Excluding topics from the output TOC

By default, every topic referenced in the ditamap will be included in the output, regardless of whether it is referenced in the hierarchy section of the map or the `reltable` section of the map.

There will be cases where a topic in your collection should not appear in the output TOC. An example may be where you have a topic containing an example, which you will reference from a concept topic. You may arrange the topic hierarchy so that the example topic is a *child* of the concept topic. You want a link to be automatically generated from parent to child, based on the hierarchy, but you don't want the example topic to appear as the sole child of the concept topic in the TOC.

To exclude the topic from the output TOC, you must set the relevant `topicref` element's `toc` attribute to no.

An example of the mark-up is:

```
<topicref
  format="dita"
  href="Reference/FeatureComparisonTable.dita"
  navtitle="Features in different versions of World
Time Pro"
  scope="local"
  type="reference"
  linking="yes"
  toc="no" />
```

If you do not want the parent-child link to automatically generate (because you want to link manually, or through a *reltable* relationship), you must set the hierarchy `topicref` element's `linking` attribute to none.

> **Note:** If you want to entirely exclude a topic included in a ditamap from the output, you should delete from the ditamap **all** `topicref` elements linking to that topic, including any in the relationship table. If you are using conditional publishing, you can set the filtering metadata attributes (such as `<topicref audience="administrator"... />`) on **all** `topicref` elements linking to the topic to be filtered during the publishing process.

Creating a Glossary of Terms

A *Glossary of Terms* is made up of multiple small `glossentry` topics, each with a structure of a term (`glossterm`) element followed by a definition (`glossdef`) element. The glossary of terms is assembled by referencing all the `glossentry` topics in a ditamap.

In DITA 1.2, instead of using the standard `topicref` element to reference the `glossentry` topics, you can use the `glossref` element. The `glossref` element is specialized from the `topicref` element, but differs in having a mandatory `keys` attribute.

The `keys` attribute is used for the automatic generation of links from terms in topic text to the corresponding glossary definition. The links are *indirect links*, in that the term in the topic links to a key, and the target of that key is defined in the ditamap. (This method of linking is known as *indirection*.)

The following code sample compares a topicref and a glossref:

```
<topicref href="mechanical/g_abs_brake_system.dita" /
>

<glossref  href="mechanical/g_brake_system.dita"
keys="abs" />
```

To specify that a link to be generated from a term to the glossary definition during publishing, you must use a `term` element, or specialized form of the *term* element named `abbreviated-form`. Both `term` and `abbreviated-form` elements have a `keyref` attribute, which is the reference to the corresponding key in the ditamap `glossref` element. (The keyref attribute was introduced in DITA 1.2.)

For example, to specify a link from the acronym *ABS* to a glossary definition of "ABS Brake System", the following code could be used:

```
<p>Your car has <abbreviated-form keyref="abs">ABS</
abbreviated-form>.
```

Except for small documents, using a separate ditamap for the glossary of terms, and then embedding the glossary ditamap in the main ditamap for the collection, is the architecture most easy to manage.

Relationship tables

Automated links based on non-hierarchical relationships are made possible through *relationship tables* (or *reltables*).

The coding for a `reltable` element within a ditamap is similar to that for a table within a topic. It is common for a reltable to have three columns: one for concept topics, one for task topics, and one for reference topics. Relationships between topics of the three information types are specified in the reltable rows.

For example, you may visualize the following reltable to associate the concept topic `c.dita` ("About Produce") with the task topic `t.dita` ("Choosing Produce") and the reference topic `r.dita` ("Available Produce"):

c.dita	t.dita	r.dita

Such a reltable would generate the following links on the "Available Produce" reference topic:

Figure 11: Example of automatically-generated links

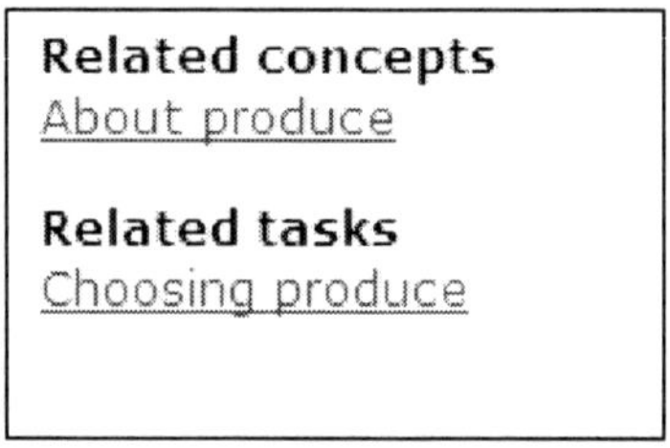

Related concepts
About produce

Related tasks
Choosing produce

By manipulating the linking characteristics of the `topicref` elements in the reltable, you can finely tune the way links are generated.

Relationship tables can technically contain nested `topicref` elements (that form a hierarchy) within a `relcell`. However, you should avoid using this sort of construct.

Types of relationship tables

There are many different ways that you can organize relationship tables. The most common are:

source and target The source column lists the topics in which a link will be included, and the target column lists the topics that the source will be linked to ("from source, to target"). Target topics do not have links back to the source topic.

task, concept, and reference Topics are organized into columns by information type. Each topic in a cell will be linked to all other topics that are in other cells in the same row. Topics in the same cell will not be linked to each other unless that cell's `collection-type` attribute is set to `family`.

task, concept, reference, and external Topics are organized into columns by information type, with an extra column for link targets that are external to the ditamap collection. Each topic in a cell will be linked to all other topics that are in other cells in the same row, and all URLs listed in the external cell in the same row. Topics in the same cell will not be linked to each other unless that cell's `collection-type` attribute is set to `family`.

Some people have found that a four column arrangement of *sourceonly task*, *targetonly concept*, *targetonly task*, and *targetonly reference* is effective.

The arrangement of the reltable is defined by the following attributes in the `relcolspec` or `rellcell` elements of the table:

linking defines the rules by which links are generated

type defines the information type (concept, task, reference, *specialized*)

scope defines whether the related information is external to the collection (typically, a Web resource)

A setting in the `relcolspec` element will cascade down to the `relcell` element.

You can also choose to have a number of relationship tables of different designs in the same ditamap. You can use the reltable's `title` attribute to label the different reltables in a map; this `title` is not used in any output, so it is only an aid to authors.

Labels for `reltable` related topic links

Generated relationship links are typically grouped, in the output, by information type. For example, links may be grouped under `Related Concepts`, `Related Tasks`, and `Related References` headings.

In a typical transformation to an output format, the wording of these headings is drawn from the (information) `type` attribute of the `topicref` element. If the `type` is not specified in the `topicref` element, the information type is determined from the topic file itself. If the `type` is not a base information type (that is, not concept, task or reference), the link is generated under a heading of "Related Information" instead.

If a referenced topic is external to the current ditamap collection (that is, it has a `scope` attribute of external), or not available at build time (that is, it has a `scope` attribute of peer), and a `type` attribute is not specified in the `topicref` element, the link will be generated under a heading of "Related Topics".

Link text for `reltable` related topic links

By default, the link text used for generated links will be the title of the target topic.

If you want the link generated by a reltable to have a different title to the title of the linked topic itself, you may think the technique would be to use a `navtitle` attribute in the `topicref` element. However, that doesn't work!

The technique to use is to add a `topicmeta` element to the `topicref`, and include a `linktext` element containing the name of the link text. The following example shows the technique.

```
<reltable>
...
  <topicref href="foo.xml">
    <topicmeta>
      <linktext>Replacement text</linktext>
    </topicmeta>
  </topicref>
...
</reltable>
```

Storing relationship tables in separate, embedded ditamaps

For collections larger than around 50 topics, it is preferable to store relationship table information in a separate ditamap file, embedded (nested) within the *master ditamap* for the collection. The relationship table map should only contain reltable sections.

For very large documents, you may choose to have multiple embedded reltable ditamaps.

Linking relationships

One of the most powerful features of DITA is the automatic generation of cross-reference links in the output. This feature allows greater content re-use, as it removes linking context from topics and moves it to the map.

Cross-reference links at the bottom of output topics are generated by hierarchical relationships defined in the ditamap, non-hierarchical relationships defined in the `reltable` section of the ditamap, and links defined in the `related-topic` section of the individual topic.

Of course, how links are generated will ultimately be up to the publishing engine you use.

The `collection-type` and `linking` attributes (of the topicref and relcell elements) allow you to fine-tune the way in which links are generated.

Hierarchical linking relationships

The hierarchy of topic references in the ditamap controls not only the sequence of topics in the output and/or the TOC, but also influences automatically-generated navigation links and generated summary content in parent topics in some output formats.

DITA permits you to adjust the basis on which the automatic navigation links are generated through the `collection-type` attribute of the `topicref` element.

Which collection type to use is dependent on the nature of the content. However, if in doubt, leave the default, which provides links to any child topics, and a link back from child to parent. This ensures that all topics in a hypertext output such as HTML can be traversed using links alone.

Relationship between hierarchy and relationship table links

Cross-reference links are automatically generated by DITA publishing tools based on the hierarchical relationships in the ditamap, and on relationship table associations in the `reltable` section of the ditamap. In addition, links can be manually specified in an individual topic in the `related-links` section of the topic.

Regardless of which linking methodology was used, the resultant links in the output are merged into categorized link blocks at the end of the topic in the output.

Figure 12: How hierarchy, reltable and related links are merged in the output topic shows a sample of links at the bottom of a topic in Microsoft HTML Help output. The `Parent topic:` link is based on the hierarchy; it is a link to the parent of the current topic. The first two `Related concepts` links are based on the ditamap hierarchy, as the parent topic has its `collection-type` attribute set to family. (This specifies that all *sibling* topics should be linked together.) The third link is a manual link specified in the `related-links` section of the current topic. These three links are all *concept* information types, and that's why they have been grouped under the `Related concepts` heading. The two `Related tasks` links are generated from a relationship in the `reltable`, again, grouped together because both topics are *task* information types.

Figure 12: How hierarchy, reltable and related links are merged in the output topic

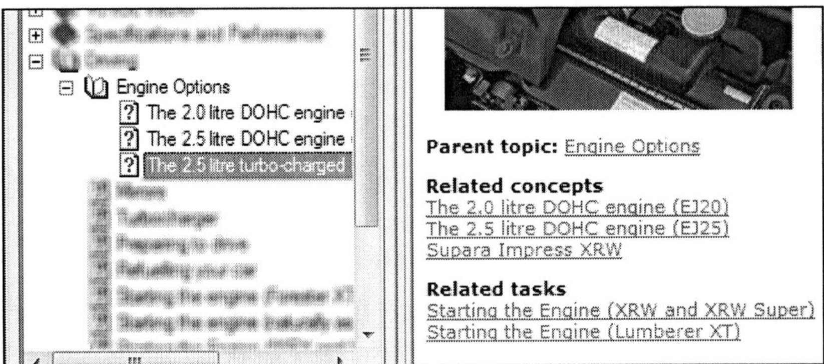

The key features of the ditamap that would generate the output in Figure 12: How hierarchy, reltable and related links are merged in the output topic are:

```
...
<topicref collection-type="family"
href="c_Engine_Options.dita" type="concept">
   <topicref href="ej20.xml" type="concept"/>
   <topicref href="ej25.xml" type="concept"/>
   <topicref href="ej25_turbo.xml" type="concept"/>
</topicref>
...
<reltable>
   <relrow>
      <relcell>
         <topicref format="dita" href="ej25_turbo.xml"
type="concept"/>
      </relcell>
      <relcell>
         <topicref format="dita" href="start_xrw.xml"
type="task"/>
            <topicref format="dita"
href="start_lumberer.xml" type="task"/>
      </relcell>
   </relrow>
</reltable>
```

Collection types

The way links are generated during output processing is dependent upon the `collection-type` attribute of *parent* `topicref` elements in the hierarchy section of the ditamap, or the containing `relcell` section in the reltable section of the ditamap. (A parent `topicref` is one containing nested `topicref` elements, or *child nodes.*) The `collection-type` therefore defines the type of hierarchical relationship between members of the same *branch* of a ditamap *tree*, or in the same cell in the relationship table `relcell` element.

There are five collection types in DITA:

unordered A collection of topics where links are generated from parent to children, and from children to parent.

family A collection of topics where links are generated from parent to children, from children to parent, and from sibling to sibling.

sequence A collection of topics where links are generated from parent to children, from children to parent, and from child to previous sibling (if applicable) and next sibling (if applicable).

choice Not commonly used, but is intended for situations where the reader needs to select one child topic to proceed. This might be useful when the output document is an interactive decision-support application. Most processors treat choice in the same way as unordered.

tree *Tree* is not supported.

Example syntax: `<topicref href="abc.dita" collection-type="sequence" />`

Although `collection-type` attributes are valid in relationship table `relcell` elements, some don't make a lot of sense in that context.

For example, setting a `collection-type` in a relationship table cell to sequence will result in a **Next Topic** link in the output linking to the next topic referenced in the cell, rather than the next topic in the TOC sequence (as may logically be expected by the reader).

Although it is possible to set a `collection-type` attribute of sequence to a `relcell` element, this is generally confusing to the user, as it will set a topic sequence that differs from the sequence of topics in the hierarchy. The same logic applies to the choice attribute value. For this reason, avoid using `collection-type` attribute values of sequence and choice. An exception is when you are creating documents with multiple sequential navigation pathways.

Likewise, a *reltable* doesn't often have parent/child relationships like the hierarchy section of the map does, so using a family `collection-type` again rarely makes sense in *reltables*.

Collection type examples

The effect of the `collection-type` attribute on the output publication is well illustrated with examples of the results of the use of different types.

Collection type example: family

Figure 13: Example of family collection type

You can save money on canned goods by:

- buying from chain or discount grocery stores
- buying larger cans

Parent topic: Shopping for groceries

Related concepts
About produce

Related tasks
Choosing produce
Buying canned goods

Related reference
Available produce
Available canned goods

Collection type example: unordered

Figure 14: Example of unordered collection type

You can save money on canned goods by:

- buying from chain or discount grocery stores
- buying larger cans

Parent topic: Shopping for groceries

Collection type example: sequence

Figure 15: Example of sequence collection type

You can save money on canned goods by:

- buying from chain or discount grocery stores
- buying larger cans

Parent topic: Shopping for groceries
Previous topic: About produce
Next topic: Choosing produce

Collection type example: choice

Figure 16: Example of choice collection type

You can save money on canned goods by:

- buying from chain or discount grocery stores
- buying larger cans

Parent topic: Shopping for groceries

The `linking` attribute

The `topicref` element (in the hierarchy section of the ditamap) and the `relcolspec` and `relcell` elements (in the reltable section of the ditamap) have a `linking` attribute. This attribute allows fine-tuning of the way in which links are automatically generated in the output publication.

The `linking` attribute values are:

targetonly A topic can only be linked to and cannot link to other topics.

sourceonly A topic cannot be linked to but can link to other topics.

normal A topic can be linked to and can link to other topics. Use this to override the linking value of a parent topic.

none A topic cannot be linked to or link to other topics.

Example syntax: `<topicref href="abc.dita" linking="sourceonly" />`

An example of the use of the `linking` attribute is in the case where you don't want the links to the parent topic to appear in each child topic. By setting the parent topic's `linking` attribute to sourceonly, the output result will show links from the parent to child topics, but not from child topics to the parent.

Similarly, if you did not want a particular branch of the ditamap hierarchy to have any generated links, you could set the parent topicref's `linking` attribute to none.

Breadcrumbs

A feature of some document delivery formats, notably Eclipse Help, is the *breadcrumb trail. Breadcrumbs* provide the user with the position of the currently displayed topic in the TOC hierarchy through links to parent and other ancestor topics.

Breadcrumbs are derived entirely from the TOC structure, and do not need to be separately defined in the DITA source.

Figure 17: TOC hierarchy used to derive breadcrumb trail in Eclipse Help output

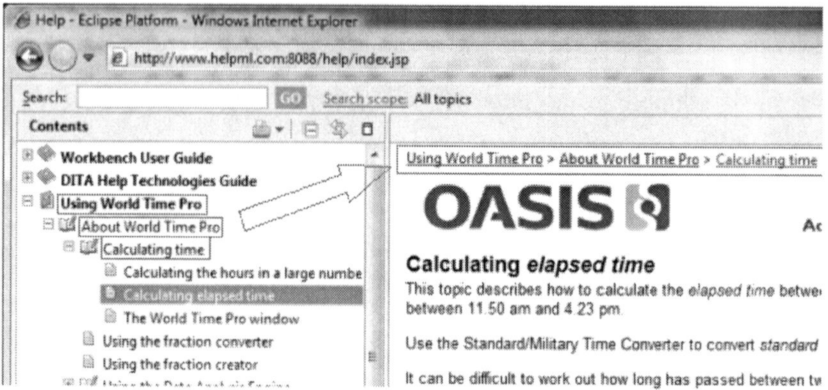

Inheritance and cascades in ditamaps

In the hierarchy section of a ditamap, attribute values in parent topicref elements *cascade* down to child elements. For example, setting an `audience` attribute of `administrator` in a parent `topicref` will result in all child topicref elements being treated, during processing to an output format, as though they also have an `audience` attribute of `administrator`. So if you want to exclude a "chapter" of a publication from an output using conditional processing, you only need to set the metadata attribute on the chapter parent `topicref` element, and not on all individual `topicref` elements.

If a conflicting attribute is set at a lower level, such as the case where a parent `product` attribute is set to `pro` and a child `product` attribute is set to `lite`, the setting on the child `topicref` will override the setting on the parent.

When you want to set attribute values for a group of topics that do not have a common parent topicref, you can use the `topicgroup` element created for this very purpose. A `topicgroup` simply serves as a non-hierarchical container for `topicref` elements in a ditamap. It has the same attributes as a `topicref` element.

Some elements and attributes in a ditamap are specifically designed to override the corresponding settings in the topic itself. For example, a navigation title (`navtitle`) attribute of the `topicref` in a ditamap will override the topic's `title` element as the source for the text to be used in the output table of contents.

Embedded (or nested) ditamaps

The `topicref` elements in a ditamap usually reference a topic. However, they can also reference ditamaps, which opens up the opportunity for having *embedded* (or *nested*) maps.

A reference to a ditamap differs from a reference to a topic in having a `format` attribute of ditamap. The syntax of a reference to a ditamap is:

```
<topicref
  format="ditamap"
   href="engine/ej25.ditamap"
   navtitle="2.5 Litre Engine">
</topicref>
```

Figure 18: Re-used, embedded (or nested) ditamaps illustrates how ditamaps (such as the *Storing Data* and *Widget Specifications* ditamaps) can be nested within another ditamap (in this case, the *Widget User Guide*). Nesting can continue down to many levels deep. And ditamaps can be nested within **many** other ditamaps.

Figure 18: Re-used, embedded (or nested) ditamaps

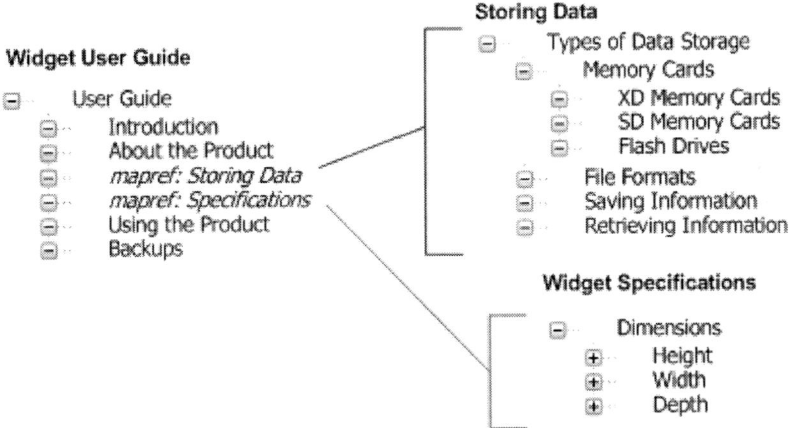

Nesting ditamaps is a useful tool in permitting content re-use and authoring efficiency.

The term *mapref* is sometimes used as shorthand for a `topicref` with a `format` attribute of ditamap. Until DITA 1.2, there was no DITA element of `mapref`, but 1.2 introduced a `mapref` as a convenience element identical in functionality to `topicref` with a `format` attribute of ditamap.

DITA map vocabulary

DITA includes a range of elements and attributes to manage references in ditamaps, and to govern the way the references are treated during the publishing process.

The `topicref` element

Topic references nominate the topic or other resource to be included in the collection. They are similar in function to a cross-reference (`xref`) element in topic content.

The `topicref` element is used for the hierarchical section of the ditamap and the relationship table section.

Resources that a `topicref` element can reference include DITA topics within the collection, (embedded) ditamaps, DITA topics external to the collection, external files, and Internet resources.

The main attributes of the `topicref` element are the `href`, `scope`, `format`, and `type` attributes.

The `href` attribute in a topic references

Topic reference (`topicref`) elements usually reference a DITA topic, but can also reference external resources such as Web sites. The resources being referenced in `topicref` element are specified in the `href` attribute.

A *URI*, or *Uniform Resource Indicator*, is a standard for referencing resources on the Internet. The similar term *URL*, or *Uniform Resource Locator*, means a specific type of *URI* where the location and the means of retrieving the resource are both incorporated in the address. For example, the *URL* `http://store.scriptorium.com/items/Books/list.htm` nominates the address of the resource and the protocol to use to retrieve it (in this case, *http*). In general, however, most people use the terms interchangeably!

Files on a file server or network drive on a local network can be referenced using the URI convention. Most DITA authoring tools will let you browse for the resource you want to reference, and then format the address in the correct UNC format. For example, the address of a file on a network server must be prefixed with the protocol `smb://`.

You must use (forward) slash characters for path separators. Do not use backslashes. Such file references are URIs in DITA, not file paths. The backslash is an illegal character in URIs. When referencing resources on a network server, prefix the UNC path with `smb://`.

You cannot use an ampersand (&) character in an `href` attribute. If the URL being referenced contains an ampersand character, the `&` character escape should be used to indicate that character.

The `topichead` element

The `topichead` element in the ditamap provides a way of creating a parent node in the hierarchy section without needing to have a corresponding topic.

You should avoid using `topichead` elements for your final ditamap. However, you might find them useful when drafting or planning your collection structure.

There are two main reasons why topichead elements should be avoided.

The first is that it conflicts with the notion of the separation of content and form, and the separation of data and metadata. All *content* (*data*) in a document should reside in the topics, not in the map. The ditamap should only contain `metadata`. If you use `topichead` as an alternative to a title-only topic, you are effectively placing non-reusable content, or data, in the ditamap.

The second reason is more practical. If you are transforming a ditamap to a hypertext output format with a TOC, such as to Eclipse Help, the `topichead` elements will be transformed to unlinked parent nodes in the TOC. When the user clicks on such a node, the content pane will not display an associated topic, as it will for other nodes in the TOC. This inconsistency appears to the user to be an error. The unlinked node in the TOC will also cause inconsistencies or malfunctions in the way breadcrumbs function, and the way sequences (previous and next topic links) function.

The `navref` element

Some Help system output formats, including Eclipse Help and Microsoft HTML Help, support *runtime merging* of modular Help files, where a *master* Help system incorporates *slave* Help system modules dynamically when the user opens the Help.

The `navref` element provides for run-time modular navigation structures. In other words, the target defined by `navref` is resolved not when the parent ditamap is being built, but when the resultant deliverable is being rendered. It is a fairly obscure element, and is not commonly used.

You may choose to use `navref` as a placeholder when you are building a document suite, where a constituent ditamap is not yet available. Even though the `navref href` is not available, the ditamap will still build. When the map referenced by the `navref` is available, the `navref` should be replaced by a normal `topicref`.

The `copy-to` attribute

You can use the `copy-to` attribute of the ditamap `topicref` element when you need the output file name to differ from what would otherwise be automatically generated, or when you need two or more identical or almost identical copies of the same topic in the output. The copies of the original topic can have different generated link text and generated short descriptions.

The value entered in the `copy-to` attribute is the duplicate file name, with a `.dita` extension. If you name the file `ej25_special.dita`, and generate to XHTML, the output file name will be `ej25_special.html`. The original topic file name will always be generated in the output; `copy-to` creates a duplicate file name, rather than modifying the file name.

The `copy-to` attribute will also let you apply different metadata attributes (even `navtitle`) for each reference in the map. For example, you could have one topic about saving data records, and use it in the ditamap twice as "Saving Customer Records" and "Saving Staff Records".

The use of the `copy-to` attribute is appropriate in both the hierarchy section of the ditamap and the reltable section.

Note: When using the DITA Open Toolkit, the file extension provided in the `copy-to` attribute must be `.xml` or `.dita`.

An example of when `copy-to` might be used to create two identical topics is as follows. A Microsoft HTML Help system is being developed, where the same topic needs to be displayed as a child of two different parent nodes in different parts of the TOC hierarchy. Microsoft HTML Help has a *synchronize TOC* function, and a sequential browsing function. If the same HTML topic is used in two different places in the TOC, the synchronize function will always highlight the first occurrence of the topic file name in the TOC pane, thus confusing the user who expects to see the topic in a different section of the Help system. Using the `copy-to` attribute to specify an alternative file name for the second instance in the DITA map file will result in two topics being generated during processing, and the synchronization and other sequencing problems will not occur in the output.

You should only use the `copy-to` attribute in `topicref` elements in relationship tables when you need to create a second output file **and** you need to alter the topic's linking or short description characteristics in the second copy.

For example, you may want the information in a topic about turbochargers to appear in the output twice, and to be referenced in the `Related Topics` link group in one instance as "XT Turbocharger Explained", but in another output topic's `Related Topics` link group as "WRX Turbocharger Explained". In this case, you would use enter the alternative linking text in a linktext element within a topicmeta element in the topicref, such as:

```
<topicref href="turbo.dita" copy-to="xrw_turbo.dita">
  <topicmeta>
    <linktext>XRW Turbocharger Explained</linktext>
  </topicmeta>
</topicref>
```

Make sure you don't use the `copy-to` attribute when you only need to change the link text; in this case, the `linktext` element can be used alone.

The `chunk` attribute

The ditamap's `topicref` element includes a `chunk` attribute that can be used to aggregate source DITA topics during processing to a deliverable document.

Setting the `chunk` attribute effectively overrides the default processing of the publishing tool. As well as specifying that multiple DITA topics be generated as single output topics, the `chunk` attribute can also be used to specify that single DITA topics be split on output into multiple output topics.

The `chunk` attribute is also available on the `map` element; values set will apply to all the topics in the ditamap.

The `chunk` attribute is only ever applied to a parent node `topicref` element or a `map` element, and its value applies to the parent and its child topics.

The `chunk` attribute has up to three parts, or *tokens*, each separated by a space. For example, an attribute coded as `chunk="select-topic to-content"` has two tokens; select-topic and to-content.

There are three categories of tokens:

Selection tokens — Selection tokens are only used for identifying nested topics within a composite ditabase topic, so that the chunking policy can be applied to an individual nested topic (select-topic), a family of nested topics (select-branch), or the entire composite topic (select-document).

Policy tokens — Policy tokens specify whether the referenced topics should be split (by-topic) or merged (by-document).

Rendering tokens — Rendering tokens specify whether the referenced topics should be generated as a single topic (to-content), or whether they should be generated as separate topics but with just one entry in the table of contents (to-navigation).

As an example, a portion of a ditamap with a structure of:

```
<topicref href="c_safety.dita" chunk="to-content">
  <topicref
```

```
href="c_electronic_brake_force_distribution.dita"  /
>
  <topicref href="t_child_restraint.dita" />
  <topicref href="c_other_restraint_systems.dita" />
</topicref>
```

will be output as one single HTML topic, with a file name of `c_safety.html`.

> **Note:** With the exception of the rendering tokens, most valid `chunk` attributes apply only to the processing of composite (*ditabase*) topics. Where possible, avoid using composite topics, and instead use ditamaps.

Non-DITA topic references

Sometimes, a deliverable document in a DITA workflow will not be made up exclusively of DITA content. For example, a user manual may need to include a PDF form, or a Web site may need to include an interactive Flash tutorial created by another party. In such cases, when specifying the ditamap (a *manifest* of content for your deliverable document), you may need to include references to non-DITA resources.

These non-DITA resources are referenced through the standard `topicref` element, but with two attributes set to nominate that the referenced files are non-DITA, and external to the project. These two attributes are `format` and `scope`. You would also normally provide a navigation title (`navtitle` attribute) and lock the title (setting the `locktitle` attribute to yes) so that the processor doesn't try to retrieve the topic from the referenced resource.

Further, you may want the TOC in the output, generated from the ditamap, to include links to Web sites or e-mail addresses. You can do this by again using the standard `topicref` element, but with the `format` attribute set to html and the `scope` attribute set to external.

The following code example shows a reference to a Web site, and a reference to a PDF file located in a folder relative to the output folder.

```
<topicref
  format="html"
  href="http://www.Supara.com.au/"
  locktitle="yes" navtitle="Supara Australia Web
Site" scope="external"/>
<topicref format="pdf" href="pdf/
```

```
2006_impre_brochure.pdf" locktitle="yes"
navtitle="Supara Impress 2006 Brochure" scope="peer"/
>
```

Valid `format` attribute values are:

dita	for DITA topics
html	for HTML or XHTML resources
pdf	for PDF documents
ditamap	for embedded ditamap files

However, the `format` attribute accepts any string, so if you are referencing another type of resource, you can use the file extension (without the "."). For example, if you are referencing a Word 2007 document, you would use `docx` as the `format` attribute value.

Valid `scope` attribute values are:

local	the resource is part of the current content collection
peer	the resource is part of the current content collection, but will not be available when the ditamap is processed (the resource will be separately created)
external	the resource is not part of the current content collection

The `scope` attribute also has an effect on what window the resource opens in (when generated to a hypertext output).

Dangling topicrefs

A *dangling topicref* is a reference in a ditamap to a topic that does not exist in the collection. If you comprehend a `topicref` to be a link, a *dangling topicref* is the same as a broken link.

You may expect that the processing process will cope gracefully with the missing reference, but that is not necessarily the case. In short, it is bad practice to have *dangling topicref* in a ditamap. A *dangling topicref* should be considered an authoring error, even though it is not, strictly speaking, an XML error.

Good file management practices will help avoid *dangling topicrefs*.

The bookmap feature

The core DITA schema includes the ditamap format (or *application*), which is suitable for describing many collections of topics. However, for some book-style collections (such as a large, paper-based Reference Manual), the standard ditamap is inadequate. Like other DITA applications, ditamaps can be specialized to meet special needs.

A specialized ditamap, called *bookmap*, is now part of the base DITA specification. The bookmap is a specialization of ditamap in the same way that concept is a specialization of topic.

Figure 19: Bookmap is a specialization of ditamap

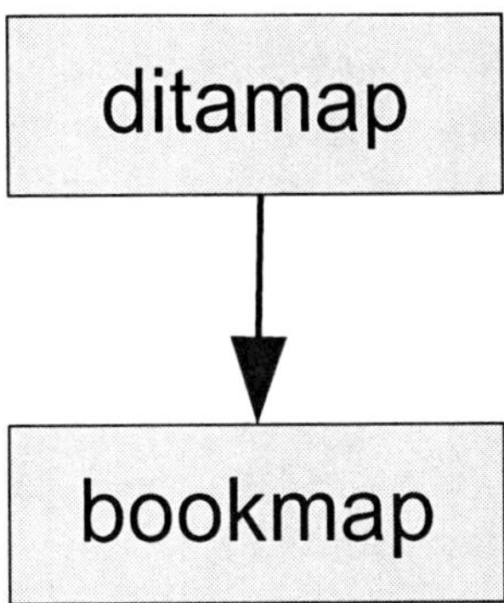

The official definition of bookmap is:

> The bookmap specialization of DITA's standard DITA map allows you to organize your DITA topics into a collection that can be printed as a book or other paged layout.
>
> **OASIS DITA Version 1.1 Architectural Specification**

Bookmap allows you to produce DITA topics as the content of a "formally defined" book. A formally defined book means one with covers, formal notices, front matter (notices, acknowledgements, dedications, preface, etc), chapters, sections, parts, and back matter (notices, lists, etc). Bookmap is needed because the standard ditamap doesn't have structures for these book components.

A bookmap has the following major structures:

- title or `booktitle`
- `bookmeta` (owners, authors, publishing data, etc)

- front matter
- any number of chapters or parts (which can contain chapters)
- any number of appendix topics
- back matter
- relationship tables.

Nesting bookmaps within ditamaps

You should not nest bookmaps within ditamaps, as the structure will cause confusion for both processing software and for documentation authors.

If you need to re-use content from a bookmap inside a ditamap, then a lower-level ditamap should be nested in the bookmap, and that lower level ditamap re-used in the main ditamap. In fact, except for small documents, you should aim to have the top-level bookmap contain only map references, and no topic references.

Sample bookmap file

```
<bookmap id="taskbook">
 <booktitle>
   <mainbooktitle>Product tasks</mainbooktitle>
   <booktitlealt>Tasks and what they do</
booktitlealt>
 </booktitle>
 <bookmeta>
   <author>John Doe</author>
   <bookrights>
     <copyrfirst>
       <year>2006</year>
     </copyrfirst>
     <bookowner>
       <person href="janedoe.dita">Jane Doe</person>
     </bookowner>
   </bookrights>
 </bookmeta>
 <frontmatter>
   <preface/>
 </frontmatter>
   <chapter format="ditamap"
href="installing.ditamap"/>
   <chapter href="configuring.dita"/>
   <chapter href="maintaining.dita">
     <topicref href="maintainstorage.dita"/>
     <topicref href="maintainserver.dita"/>
```

```
    <topicref href="maintaindatabase.dita"/>
   </chapter>
 <appendix href="task_appendix.dita"/>
</bookmap>
```

Chapter 3: Syntax and mark-up

What's in this chapter?

- Organization of DITA elements
- Working with mark-up
- Element domains
- Short descriptions
- Lists
- Paragraphs
- Procedures and steps
- Tables
- Phrases
- Special characters and dates

> I ascribe a basic importance to the phenomenon of language. To speak means to be in a position to use a certain syntax, to grasp the morphology of this or that language, but it means above all to assume a culture, to support the weight of a civilization.
>
> **Frantz Faron**

Organization of DITA elements

DITA elements can be broadly categorized as follows:

- topic elements
- map elements
- body elements
- prolog elements
- domain elements
- specialization elements

In fact, this is how the *DITA Language Reference* groups DITA elements. This categorization of the various elements is partly to aid understanding, and partly to make it technically easier for the schema files (DTD and XSD) to be managed.

Elements used within topics can also be differently categorized as block or phrase elements.

Block and phrase elements

Block elements are paragraph-like elements that are typically displayed in the output with space above and below the content, taking up the full width of the available space. Phrase (or *inline*) elements are applied to words or phrases within a block element, and typically do not force new lines in the output.

Block elements can exist within other block elements, but not within phrase elements.

Phrase elements can exist within block elements and within other phrase elements.

Examples of block elements include:

- `p` (paragraph)
- `codeblock`
- `steps`
- `msgblock`
- `title`

Examples of phrase elements include:

- `term`
- `codeph`
- `uicontrol`
- `msgph`
- `tm` (trademark)

Topic elements

The topic elements are the main structural elements of topics. Some topic elements are generic (ie, inherited from the *topic* proto information type), while others are specific to the concept, task or reference information types.

Examples of topic elements include:

- topic (and concept, task, reference, glossentry)
- titlealts
- shortdesc
- body (and refbody, conbody, taskbody, glossBody)
- section
- example
- related-links

Map elements

The map elements are a small set of elements, some of which have been specialized into other elements for use in bookmaps.

The map elements include:

- map
- topicref
- topicmeta
- topicgroup
- topichead
- reltable

Body elements

Body elements are the most common content authoring block elements, and include:

- paragraph
- list
- phrase
- figure

Prolog elements

The DITA prolog elements contain the main metadata for a topic or collection.

The types of information recorded in the prolog include:

- author
- copyright information

- critical tracking dates
- permissions for use/management of the content
- extensive metadata about the content of the document

Domain elements

Remembering that DITA started life within IBM as a tool for creating software and hardware documentation, it shouldn't be a surprise to discover that DITA's base elements reflect that background.

Elements that relate to a particular field (such as software) are called *domain elements*. The domain elements within DITA are grouped into:

typographical elements	generic word-processor like elements used to highlight text
programming elements	terms and structures related to programming environments
software elements	terms and structures related to the operation of a software program
table elements	elements that relate to table structures
user interface elements	terms and structures related to a software user interface
utilities elements	elements that don't fit anywhere else!

If you are writing a programmer's reference, you will mainly use elements in the programming domain.

If you are writing a mobile phone user guide, you should avoid using programming domain elements, and mainly use user interface domain elements.

The typographical domain elements are designed to be used only when **no semantically-appropriate elements are available** and a formatting effect is required. These elements should therefore only be used as a last resort.

Specialization elements

The DITA specialization elements are those that are used for architectural purposes rather than for semantic mark-up. In many cases, they are elements provided so that new elements can be specialized from them.

Specialization elements include:

- boolean
- data
- data-about
- foreign
- index-base
- unknown

Working with mark-up

There are a number of concepts and principles of XML mark-up in general, and DITA mark-up in particular.

Element IDs

The `id` attribute of elements must be unique in the context of a file, but ideally, should also be unique in the context of a publication. Many authoring tools automatically generate unique identifiers for elements using a *GUID*. The `id` attribute is used in referencing, such as cross-references (`xref`) and content references (`conref`).

ID attributes in DITA must start with an alphabetical character, and cannot start with a numerical character. The XML rules for ID attributes require them to start with a letter or an underscore (or a colon).

ID attributes are mandatory for the topic root elements (`topic`, `concept`, `task` and `reference`), but are optional for most other elements.

If you are going to exchange DITA documents with others, you must ensure that the interchanged document set has unique identifiers; this may require the establishment of naming conventions to avoid identifier conflicts.

Example of a generated (GUID) `id` attribute:

```
<concept
id="concept_F544B5D5759746C2A199A99518FA1EAE">
```

Examples of manually created `id` attributes:

```
<concept id="c9119">
```

```
<cite id="cite_chicago_manual_of_style_ed4">
```

Titles

The intention of the DITA approach is that the elements most commonly cross-referenced, such as topics, sections, figures and tables, should have a title. In some cases, the title element is mandatory.

Even though the DITA DTD may technically allow multiple titles to exist in one section, you should limit your section content to one title. Do not use titles as though they are headings. If you need multiple headings in a section, chances are that you really need multiple sections.

Hacks

Do not corrupt the semantics of a topic or document to achieve a formatting outcome. This is known as *tag abuse.*

For example, don't use tables for formatting only. Don't use a combination of elements, such as `cite` within `codeblock`, so that custom processing rules can be set up for a particular formatting objective.

Comments, `draft-comment`, and `required-cleanup` elements

Standard XML comment mark-up can be incorporated in DITA documents, because DITA documents are, of course, XML documents. XML comments are delimited by a `<!--` prefix and a `-->` suffix.

An example of an XML comment is:

```
<p>The kerb weight of the vehicle is 1395 kg.</p>
<!-- Check this is the correct kerb weight for XRW
model -->
```

The `draft-comment` phrase element is a DITA-specific alternative to the XML comment, and has a similar purpose.

Use the `draft-comment` element or XML comment if you want to leave comments or notes for other authors. You should prefer the `draft-comment` element to XML comment, because it is possible to deliberately include draft-comment content in the output for document review and editing.

An example of a draft-comment is:

```
<p>The kerb weight of the vehicle is 1395 kg.
<draft-comment>Check this is the correct kerb weight
for XRW model</draft-comment>
</p>
```

The required-cleanup block element is used during the migration of legacy (pre-DITA) content to DITA, to allow what would otherwise be invalid mark-up to be preserved during conversion. It is most commonly used by automatic conversion processes, such as the H2D HTML to DITA transformation provided in the DITA Open Toolkit.

The required-cleanup element can contain any well-formed mark-up.

Do not use the required-cleanup element for any purpose other than identifying invalid DITA mark-up that needs to be corrected.

Use of class attribute

All DITA elements have a class attribute, but as a DITA author, you should never change this attribute. In fact, most DITA editors will hide it from you. The DITA class attribute is not the same as the HTML class attribute. (DITA's outputclass attribute is the closest equivalent to HTML class.)

All DITA based processors use the class attribute to determine how an element should be processed, rather than by using the element name itself. This is because specialization may make the element name unfamiliar to the processor, but the class will indicate the element's inheritance, and therefore how it should be handled.

Similar element names

DITA includes a keyword element, as well as a kwd element. It includes a var element, as well as a varname element.

The reason for this apparent duplication is that DITA base elements are organized into *domains* of:

- programming
- software
- user interface
- typographical (or highlighting)

Different domains make it easier to identify elements relating to different types of documentation. In different documents, some similar concepts (such as keywords) have different semantic meanings. The differences between the apparently duplicated elements, according to the *DITA Language Reference*, are as follows.

Element	**Domain**	**Meaning**
`var`	Programming	Within a syntax diagram, the `var` element defines a variable for which the user must supply content, such as their user name or password.
`varname`	Software	The `varname` element defines a variable that must be supplied to a software application. The variable name element is very similar to the `var` element, but variable name is used outside of syntax diagrams.
`kwd`	Programming	The `kwd` element defines a keyword within a syntax diagram. A keyword must be typed or output, either by the user or application,

Element	Domain	Meaning
		exactly as specified in the syntax definition.
`keyword`	No particular domain; is used in the body and prolog.	`keyword` represents a word or phrase with special significance in a particular domain. In the general case, `keyword` elements typically do not have any special semantics and processing associated with them, but can still be useful for organizing content for re-use or special processing. Topic description keywords are typically used for searching, retrieval and classification purposes.

Controlling the look-and-feel of the output

The `outputclass` attribute can be used to specify a particular formatting characteristic during processing to an output deliverable document. Nearly all DITA content elements have an `outputclass` attribute.

For example, if you want one paragraph to be formatted differently in the output, you could use the attribute as shown in the mark-up:

```
<p>You need outside mirrors...</p>
<p outputclass="red_highlight">Your car's
mirrors...</p>
```

When generating HTML output, the DITA source `outputclass` attribute value will be generated as an HTML CSS `class` attribute.

Normally, the semantic difference between elements should drive formatting, rather than arbitrary and subjective application of `outputclass` attributes. You should therefore use the `outputclass` attribute only as a last resort.

For example, if a paragraph (`p`) element needs to be formatted differently because the paragraph contains a note or tip, the `note` element, which will be formatted differently to the standard paragraph in the output, should be used, without any need for the `outputclass` attribute.

Attaching data to content

Despite the name, the `data` element is for metadata stored in the flow of the content within the topic body. It is most useful as the basis for specializing other elements.

Within base DITA, you would most likely use the `data` element to store information about the source of code fragments, citations, or quotations. However, it is not a commonly used element.

The `data` element can be nested inside many DITA elements. Other `data` elements can be nested inside a `data` element. A `data-about` element can also be nested inside a `data` element. The `data` element has a number of attributes, including:

name the unique name for the piece of data

value the value of the piece of data

href a link to the resource used for the piece of data

For example, the detailed source of a long quotation is contained in `data` elements in the following sample:

```
<lq reftitle="Lynch and Horton (2009)" href="http://
webstyleguide.com/">
  <data name="ref_Lynch_Horton">
    <data name="date_retrieved" value="13 September
2009" />
    <data name="chapter" value="9" />
    <data name="pub_type" value="web" />
    <data name="page_URL" href="http://
webstyleguide.com/wsg3/9-editorial-style/2-
structuring-prose.html" />
    <data name="pub_title">Web Style Guide</data>
```

```
    <data name="edition" value="3" />
  </data>
The inverted pyramid style used in journalism works
well on web
pages...
</lq>
```

How the metadata stored in the `data` element structure is used is up to the authoring and publishing tools used.

Element domains

The base DITA elements are grouped into *domains*. You can see this clearly in the *DITA Language Reference*.

The DITA element mark-up domains are:

- programming
- user interface
- software
- utilities
- metadata
- typographic

Different sets of elements are intended for use when documenting different types of things. The software domain, for example, contains the elements designed to semantically describe software characteristics.

The element domains are technically organized into different DTD or XSD schema modules.

Programming domain

The elements in the programming domain are designed for documenting programming languages.

Programming domain elements

Element Name	Semantic Purpose
apiname	API name
codeblock	code block

Element Name	Semantic Purpose
codeph	code phrase
option	one of a set of options
parmname	parameter or argument
parml	parameter list
plentry	parameter list entry (within parml)
pt	parameter term (within plentry)
pd	parameter definition (within plentry)
synph	syntax phrase
syntaxdiagram	syntax diagram
groupseq	group of syntactic units (used only for syntax diagrams)
groupchoice	choice of a group of syntactic units (used only for syntax diagrams)
groupcomp	group of composite syntactic units (used only for syntax diagrams)
fragment	fragment of syntax (used only for syntax diagrams)
fragref	cross-reference to a fragment of syntax
synblk	block of small pieces of syntax
synnote	footnote within syntax (syntax note)
synnoteref	cross-reference to a syntax note
kwd	syntax keyword (used only for syntax diagrams)
var	variable that a user must supply (used only for syntax diagrams)
oper	operator character (such as +, -, and =) within syntax
delim	delimiter character (such as /, |, and ;) within syntax
sep	separator character within syntax
repsep	separator character for repeated syntax elements

User interface domain

The user interface domain elements are designed for documenting the user interface of a software program.

User interface domain elements

Element Name	Semantic Purpose
uicontrol	user interface control
wintitle	window title
menucascade	menu cascade
shortcut	shortcut
screen	character (text only) screen

Software domain

The software domain elements are designed for documenting the operation of a software program.

Software domain elements

Element Name	Semantic Purpose
msgph	message phrase
msgblock	message block
msgnum	message number
cmdname	command name
varname	variable (to be provided by user) name
filepath	file name or path, or URI
userinput	user input
systemoutput	system output

Utilities domain

The utilities domain elements are non-semantic elements used in defining image maps.

Utilities domain elements

Element Name	Semantic Purpose
imagemap	client-side image map
area	hotspot area within an image map
coords	co-ordinates of a hotspot area within an image map
shape	shape of a hotspot area within an image map

Metadata domain

The metadata domain elements are designed for describing index entries and map-level metadata elements.

Metadata domain elements

Element Name	Semantic Purpose
index-see	redirection to another index entry
index-see-also	additional redirection to another index entry
index-sort-as	alternative sort phrase for an index entry
topicgroup	non-hierarchical group of topics in a ditamap
topichead	title only heading entry in a ditamap
authorinformation	author information (in a bookmap)
addressdetails	address details (in a bookmap)
administrativearea	address county, state, province or other administrative area within address details (in a bookmap)
contactnumber	contact telephone number within a group of contact numbers (in a bookmap)
contactnumbers	group of contact telephone numbers within address details (in a bookmap)
country	address country within address details (in a bookmap)
emailaddresses	group of e-mail addresses within address details (in a bookmap)

Element Name	Semantic Purpose
emailaddress	e-mail address within a group of e-mail addresses (in a bookmap)
firstname	first or given name within name details (in a bookmap)
generationidentifier	generation identifier within name details (in a bookmap)
honorific	honorific within name details (in a bookmap)
lastname	last or family name within name details (in a bookmap)
locality	locality or city within address details (in a bookmap)
localityname	locality name within locality (in a bookmap)
middlename	middle name within name details (in a bookmap)
namedetails	name details within organization information (in a bookmap)
organizationinfo	organization information (in a bookmap)
organizationname	organization name within organization name details (in a bookmap)
organizationnamedetails	organization name details within name details (in a bookmap)
otherinfo	other information within organization name details (in a bookmap)
personinfo	person information (in a bookmap)
personname	person name within name details (in a bookmap)
postalcode	postal code or zip code within locality (in a bookmap)
thoroughfare	street, road, or other thoroughfare within address details (in a bookmap)
url	URL or URI within a group of URLs (in a bookmap)
urls	group of URLs or URIs within organization details (in a bookmap)

Typographic (highlighting) domain

The elements in the typographic domain are used to describe styling characteristics. They are primarily intended as the basis for specialization. Avoid using these elements.

Semantic elements should always be used in preference to typographic elements.

Typographic domain elements

Element Name	Semantic Purpose
b	bold (strong)
i	italic (emphasis)
u	underlined
tt	teletype (typewriter)
sup	superscript
sub	subscript

Short descriptions

Short descriptions serve multiple purposes within a document. This is one of the reasons that it is difficult to categorise `shortdesc` as content (data) or metadata. Technically, `shortdesc` is metadata because it falls outside the topic `body` element.

To complicate matters further, DITA includes a semantically similar element, the `abstract`, which serves a similar function (and can act as an alternative) to `shortdesc`.

Writing short descriptions induces the writer to clarify the main thesis of the topic. If you cannot write a short description of within the recommended 50 word limit, the topic is probably too complex and needs to be divided. If the short description doesn't add any meaning to the topic, then the topic may not contain a coherent idea.

A concise and complete short description should be written for every DITA topic.

Purpose of short descriptions

The short description (`shortdesc`) element allows a writer to provide a short overview of the content of the topic. The `shortdesc` is typically generated as the first content paragraph (after the title) in the output. However, some processors can omit the short description from the topic entirely. The `shortdesc` is also typically used for link previews (in hypertext output formats), and for subordinate topic preview summaries in parent topics. Again, some processors may not generate the `shortdesc` elements in this way. Some processors may also truncate the short description in a link preview or subordinate topic preview.

Figure 20: Example of short descriptions as subordinate topic previews in HTML output

the label and, if GST applies, a default GST amount of 10%. You can change this amount if necessary.

Learn more:

To create a label
Creating a label involves entering a descriptive name and specifying the tax code that should apply to transactions with this label.

To delete a label
You can delete a label without affecting any transactions.

To edit a label
You can edit the name and tax code of a label, but this does not affect any transactions.

Figure 21: Example of short description as link previews in HTML output

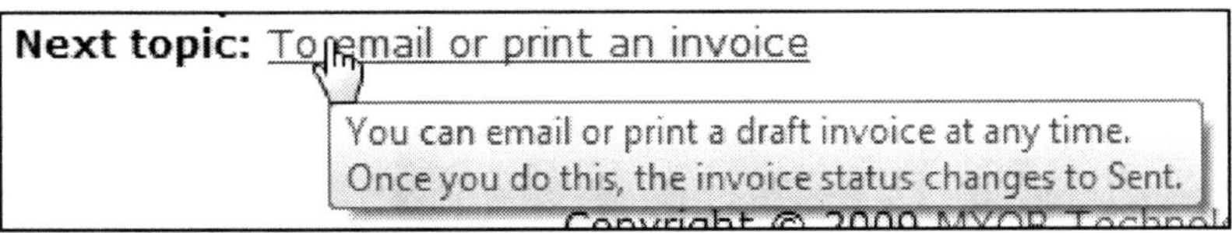
Next topic: To email or print an invoice
You can email or print a draft invoice at any time.
Once you do this, the invoice status changes to Sent.

Short descriptions can be defined in the topic, or in the `topicmeta` section of the `topicref` in the ditamap.

The short description should normally be defined in the topic. Only if the topic has a different purpose in a particular ditamap should the short description be defined in the map.

Subordinate topic previews and link previews serve as *progressive disclosure devices*, which aim to provide the reader with an understanding of what the linked topic contains, without having to follow the link. This allows the user to navigate through the online document more efficiently.

As the first paragraph of the topic, the short description can serve as an overview that allows the reader to quickly decide whether to read on. This purpose is more readily achieved by the systematic use of short descriptions, and visually identifying the short description in the output with distinctive styling (thematic unity).

Figure 22: Example of short description styled distinctively in HTML output

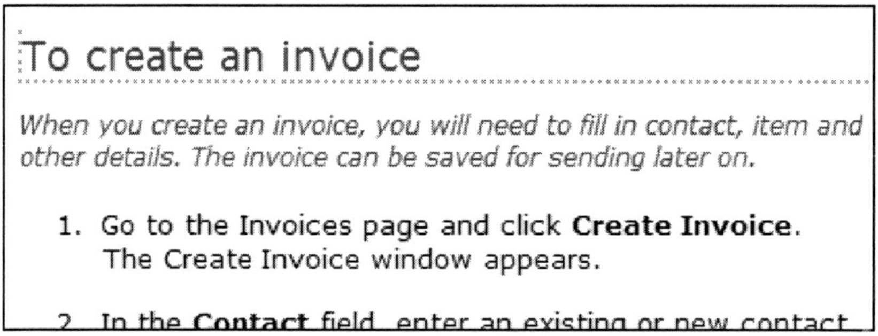

To create an invoice

When you create an invoice, you will need to fill in contact, item and other details. The invoice can be saved for sending later on.

1. Go to the Invoices page and click **Create Invoice**. The Create Invoice window appears.
2. In the **Contact** field, enter an existing or new contact

Guidelines for crafting short descriptions

This table is a summary of the recommendations made by Kris Eberlein in her *Art of the Short Description* presentation at the 2007 DITA Europe Conference.

Do:	Don't
• Make the `shortdesc` *standalone*, so that the topic is not dependent upon the `shortdesc`. • Make the `shortdesc` concise and complete. • Include less than 50 words in only one or two sentences. • Use complete sentences, except for short topics such as in API documentation.	• Restate the title. • State the obvious. • Start the `shortdesc` with "this topic...". • Use the `shortdesc` as a lead-in sentence.

Different approaches to writing short descriptions are required for different information types.

Information Type	Guidelines
Task	The `shortdesc` should answer the questions of what are the benefits of the task, and what is the purpose of the task. Include information about when the user should perform the task (or why the task is necessary). If applicable, include information about who performs the task.
Concept	The `shortdesc` should answer the questions of what is this, and why do I care about this. Start with a brief definition, if the concept is unfamiliar. Make sure the `shortdesc` contains the main point of the topic.
Reference	The `shortdesc` should answer the questions of what are the items, what do they do, and what are they used for. Use consistent phrasing across document sets so that your information can be easily integrated into a range of publications.

Abstracts

The `abstract` element is similar to the `shortdesc` element, in that it is used to contain a concise summary of the content of the topic. Abstracts should be used for special cases only, as they only offer advantages over short descriptions in limited scenarios.

DITA `abstract` elements are similar to short descriptions, but allow for more complex information structures. An abstract can contain a range of block elements such as paragraphs and notes, but can also contain one or more `shortdesc` elements.

A topic can contain either an `abstract` (which may include a nested `shortdesc`), or a standalone `shortdesc`, but not both.

In general, a `shortdesc` should be used in preference to an `abstract`, following the principle that the simplest approach is usually the best.

The `abstract` structure should be used for:

- topics where multiple short descriptions are needed because the topic is to be conditionally published
- re-use topics, where multiple `shortdesc` elements are going to be *conreffed* into other topics
- complex topics where the `shortdesc` is too limited to adequately summarise the topic content.

Only the `shortdesc` element(s) within the `abstract` are included in the topic previews and link previews.

Cross-references and typography in `shortdesc` elements

At first glance, the `shortdesc` element seems unable to contain some inline mark-up such as cross-references. On closer examination, it becomes apparent that a `ph` inline element can be inserted, and that `ph` element can contain cross-references.

Although the DITA language technically permits this sort of mark-up construct, hacks such as this should not be used.

Example of invalid code:

```
<shortdesc>The <xref href="c_turbo.dita#c4753/
turbo_overview">
turbocharger systems</xref> uses...
```

Example of technically valid, but unwise, code:

```
<shortdesc>The <ph><xref href="c_turbo.dita#c4753/
turbo_overview">
turbocharger systems</xref></ph> uses...
```

The `shortdesc` element is intended to contain a brief synopsis of the content of the topic, and isn't necessarily intended to be output as part of the topic content. It is intended for link previews and hover text; it doesn't make sense to include cross-references in these.

In the same way, typographical elements such as bold (`b`) and italic (`i`) are not usually appropriate in short descriptions, even though they are technically valid, because short descriptions are often rendered in plain text forms (such as in tooltips). If you think you need such formatting, you should consider whether the content you are including really belongs in a `shortdesc` element.

The shortdesc should be treated as metadata, not content.

A `shortdesc` may legitimately need some inline mark-up, such as where a superscript or subscript character is needed. For example, a `shortdec` might discuss water as `H<sub>2</sub>O`. This will inevitably present a problem when the `shortdesc` text is used in a context where subscripts are not permitted, such as in a tooltip or an HTML topic title.

Inline mark-up in a `shortdesc` should therefore be avoided where the formatting of that mark-up in the output is important to its meaning.

Making `shortdesc` elements compulsory

Some publications managers may wish to make the use of `shortdesc` mandatory within a DITA authoring team. To make such an element mandatory in DITA, specialization or constraints have to be used. (Some authoring tools also allow configuration independently of DITA to make elements mandatory.)

In specialization, the schema designer creates a new information type (for example, `myconcept`), with `shortdesc` defined as a required element within that information type. (The `shortdesc` doesn't have to be renamed under this approach.)

Using constraints (DITA 1.2 and above), the base topic element (for example, `concept`) is provided with an override rule to make the structure stricter in that the `shortdesc` element becomes mandatory.

Short descriptions in the ditamap

A short description (`shortdesc`) element naturally belongs in the topic. The short description is typically rendered in the output as:

- the first paragraph of the topic
- link preview text (in hypertext outputs)
- subordinate topic preview text in the topic's parent

In some circumstances, you may want to override the subordinate topic preview text with a publication-specific, alternative short description. To do this, you need to specify the alternative short description in the ditamap. This is done by adding a `shortdesc` element to the `topicmeta` element within the *topicref.*

An example of the topicref mark-up is:

```
<topicref href="c_starting_xrw.dita" format="dita">
  <topicmeta>
    <shortdesc>The XRW is started by entering the
PIN into the security
    keypad, and then turning the ignition key.</
shortdesc>
  </topicmeta>
</topicref>
```

> **Note:** Setting a `linktext` element within the *topicref's* `topicmeta` will similarly result in the generated hierarchical links in hypertext output using this alternative link text, rather than the topic's title.

Lists

Types of lists

The four list types in base DITA are:

Simple Lists
A simple list (`sl`) is one where the items in the list are short phrases, and where the order of items in the list is not important. The list is usually rendered with each item on a separate line, without bullets or numbers.

Bulleted (unordered) Lists
An unordered list (`ul`) is one where the order of items in the list is not important. The list is usually rendered with bullets against each list item. The items are typically blocks of text.

Numbered (ordered) Lists
An ordered list (`ol`) is one where the order of items is critical to the meaning. The list is usually rendered with sequential numbers against the list items.

Definition Lists
A definition list (`dl`) is one comprising a set of terms and corresponding definitions. The list is usually rendered with definitions indented from the term and on the next line, or with definitions indented from the term on the same line as the term.

These lists are semantically distinct, although the difference between a simple list and an unordered list is minor. Some processors may output simple lists as inline lists, rather than block lists (separate lines per item).

List types are not interchangeable; the content of the list will determine which list type is appropriate for it. Choose a list type by considering the nature of the list, not by the way you think the list will be rendered in the output.

Figure 23: The difference between simple and unordered lists

The Supara Impress range includes two turbo-charged models:

XRW
XRW Super

simple list

The Supara Impress range includes two turbo-charged models:

- XRW
- XRW Super

unordered list

Figure 24: The difference between definition and unordered lists

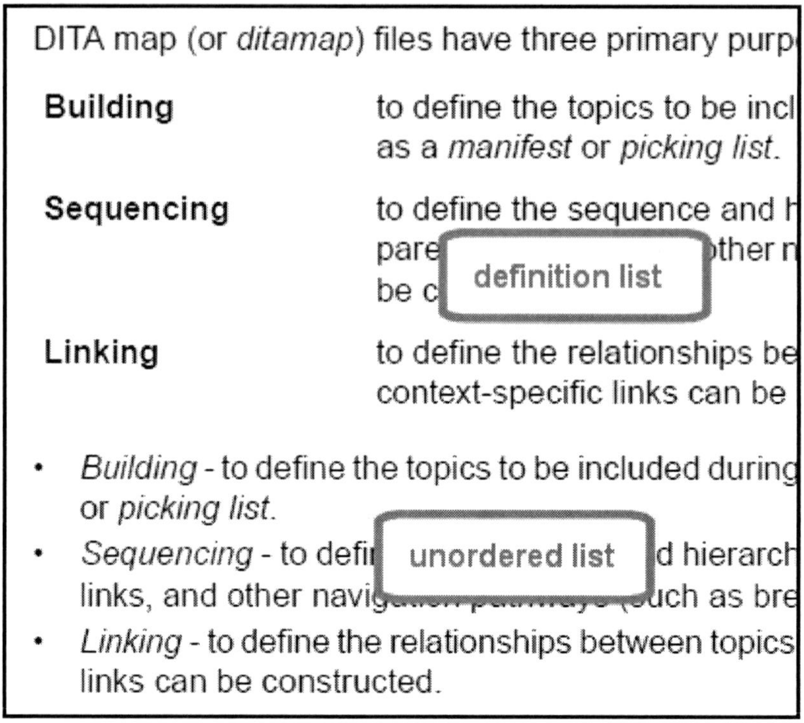

DITA map (or *ditamap*) files have three primary purp

Building to define the topics to be incl as a *manifest* or *picking list*.

Sequencing to define the sequence and h pare ther n be c

definition list

Linking to define the relationships be context-specific links can be

- *Building* - to define the topics to be included during or *picking list*.
- *Sequencing* - to defi d hierarch links, and other navi uch as bre
- *Linking* - to define the relationships between topics links can be constructed.

unordered list

Although simple lists are technically valid inside ordered, unordered and definition list items, you should avoid nesting simple lists inside other lists.

DITA includes some other special purpose list structures, such as parameter list (`parml`) and choice list (`choices`).

Definition lists versus tables

Some information structures, particularly terms with corresponding definitions, can be marked up as either definition lists or tables.

If the content is indeed made up of terms and definitions, the definition list (`dl`) structure should be used. For content not so clearly identifiable as terms and definitions, but where there is a two part structure made up of short phrase and a longer explanation of the phrase, the simpler definition list structure should always be preferred over the table structure.

Definition lists are particularly suited to defining or explaining components or items.

Figure 25: The difference between tables and definition lists

Unordered
A collection of topics where links are generated from pa children to parent.

Family
A collection of topics where links are generated from p children to pa sibling.

Sequence
A collection o nerated from p children to parent, and from child to previous sibling (if a (if applicable).

Choice
TBA. Similar to *unordered*. (A collection of topics where parent to children, and from children to parent.)

Tree
Tree is not supported.

definition list

Collection Type	Description
Unordered	A collection of topics wher parent to children, and fr
Family	A collection of topics wher parent to children, from ch sibling to sibling.
Sequence	A collection of topics wher parent to children, from ch child to previous sibling (i sibling (if applicable).
Choice	TBA. Similar to *unordere* where links are generate and from children to pare
Tree	*Tree* is not supported.

table

Definition lists are rendered with fewer potential complications than tables, and are semantically stronger than the more generic table structure.

Lists within paragraphs

DITA permits you to use a structure for a list of items where the list exists within a paragraph element. You can alternatively create a list structure without a surrounding paragraph. In other words, both of the following are valid.

```
<p>
 <ul>
```

```
  <li>Point 1</li>
  <li>Point 2</li>
 </ul>
</p>
```

and

```
<ul>
 <li>Point 1</li>
 <li>Point 2</li>
</ul>
```

The best choice is the structure that is semantically correct, and that will depend upon the context.

In most cases, the second option (a standalone list structure) is correct semantically, because most lists do not logically fall within a paragraph, and cannot be logically be surrounded by a paragraph. Further, if the paragraph has no content other than the list, then it is probably superfluous.

However, in some cases, the list may logically belong within the same idea as the surrounding paragraph. In such cases, there will be text within the paragraph element before and/or after the list element. For example:

```
<p>The four turbo-charged models are:
 <sl>
  <sli>XRW</sli>
  <sli>XRW Super</sli>
  <sli>Lumberer XT</sli>
  <sli>Liberty GT.</sli>
 </sl>
 </p>
```

A more complex example is:

```
<p>The four turbo-charged models
 <sl>
 <sli>XRW</sli>
  <sli>XRW Super</sli>
  <sli>Lumberer XT</sli>
  <sli>Liberty GT</sli>
 </sl>
 are the most expensive of their makes.</p>
```

When considering content re-use, the paragraph in the preceding example could be re-used, and would always include the list, as it is part of the same idea. The list could also be re-used without the paragraph text. But the paragraph text could not be re-used without the list.

Some people treat lead-in sentences, or stem sentences, in the same way. If a stem sentence ends with a colon, then it should only be re-used with the list it supports. Therefore, the stem sentence and the list should be in the same semantic element.

Figure 26: Comparison between parallel and embedded lists

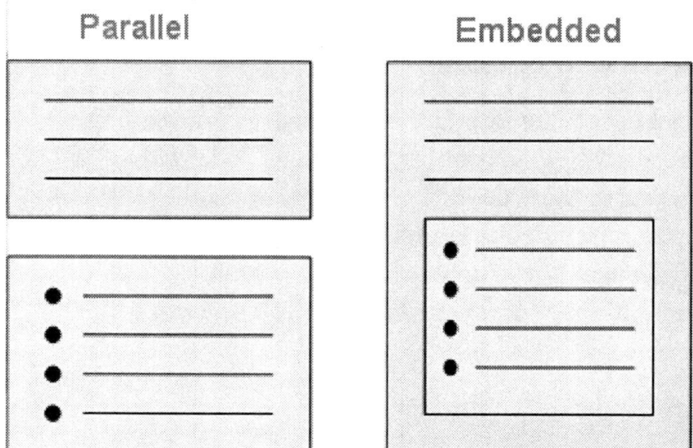

> **Note:** There are some conflicting requirements when the content needs to be localized. Including a block nested inside a paragraph, such as in the preceding examples, will create some problems for translators. This creates a dilemma which may eventually be solved by advancements in software tools. If you are writing for translation, you avoid including text after a nested block inside another block element. The guidelines contained in the *Best Practice for Leveraging Legacy Translation Memory when Migrating to DITA (Joseph & Raya, 2007)* whitepaper produced by the OASIS DITA Translation Subcommittee should be followed when writing for translation.

Controlling number (enumeration) type

By default, most DITA publishing tools render simple lists without bullets or numbers, unordered lists with bullets, numbered lists with Arabic numbers, and definition lists with the definition term as a hanging indent.

Second and subsequent level numbers in a nested ordered list are typically rendered following the format of `1. a. i..`

If an alternative enumeration scheme is required, the processing routines must be modified. There is no specific enumeration type setting in DITA, as list presentation is considered to be form, not content.

If a particular list needs to be presented differently from other lists using the same list element, the `outputclass` attribute may be used in conjunction with customized processing routines.

Listing user interface buttons

When describing a list of user interface items (such as buttons), the definition list construct is semantically appropriate. A definition list (`dl`) element contains one or more definition entry (`dlentry`) elements, each typically containing a definition term (`dt`) and a definition description (`dd`) element. If you are explaining a button, control, or any other graphic, you can insert an image in the definition term (`dt`) element.

An example of such a definition list is:

```
<dl>
 <dlentry>
  <dt><image href="sample_button.png" /></dt>
  <dd>Opens the directory associated with the
document folder.</dd>
 </dlentry>
</dl>
```

In some cases, such as when describing buttons that can be chosen within a step of a task, the `choicetable` element may be more appropriate. In other cases, especially when the structure of the content is more complex than just image and description, a table may be used.

Parameter lists

Parameter lists are a special purpose list used to describe parameters in a program or application programming interface. The parameter list (`parml`) is similar in structure to the general purpose definition list (`dl`).

A parameter list (`parml`) element contains one or more parameter list entry (`plentry`) elements, each typically containing a parameter name or term (`pt`) and a parameter description (`pd`) element.

An example of a parameter list being used to explain some programming code is:

```
<codeblock>callHelp(hFilename, contentId)</codeblock>
<p>where
<parml>
 <plentry>
  <pt>hFileName</pt>
  <pd>is the relative path to the Help file</pd>
 </plentry>
 <plentry>
  <pt>contentId</pt>
  <pd>is the context ID of the topic to display</pd>
 </plentry>
</parml>
</p>
```

Choice lists

A choice list is a special purpose list used within `step` elements in task topics to indicate that the user has to choose one of several actions to complete the task.

The choice list (`choices`) is similar in structure to the general purpose unordered list (`ul`). A `choices` element contains one or more `choice` elements.

An example of a choice list being used within a step is:

```
<step>
  <cmd>Place the car in gear.</cmd>
  <choices>
    <choice>For automatic gearboxes, select
<uicontrol>Park</uicontrol>.</choice>
    <choice>For manual gearboxes, select first
gear.</choice>
  </choices>
</step>
```

Paragraphs

Keeping connected blocks together

When one block of text leads into a second block of text, the blocks become interdependent. A risk exists that if only one of the paragraphs is re-used, it will read out of context.

For example, you may introduce a code sample with a stem sentence; the stem sentence is in a paragraph (`p`) block, and the code sample is in a logically subordinate `codeblock` block.

```
<p>The following code example shows how JavaScript
can be used in a link to print the current page:</p>
<codeblock>
&lt;a href="#" onclick="window.print()"&gt;
 Print this page
&lt;/a&gt;
</codeblock>
```

If the stem sentence paragraph is re-used outside the current topic, the text won't make sense unless the following `codeblock` travels with it. Alternatively, a conref push may inject another block between the first (`p`) block and the second (`codeblock`) block, affecting the meaning of the stem sentence.

As the two blocks are logically connected, the codeblock should be nested within the paragraph. The resultant code is:

```
<p>The following code example shows how JavaScript
can be used in a link to print the current page:
<codeblock>
&lt;a href="#" onclick="window.print()"&gt;
 Print this page
&lt;/a&gt;
</codeblock></p>
```

Examples of content structures where nesting of subordinate blocks is common include:

paragraphs within long quotes	`<lq>`
	`  <p>The was movement at the station...</p>`
	`  <p>That the colt from Old Regret...</p>`
	`</lq>`

long quotes within paragraphs	`<p>Banjo Patterson started the work with:`
	`  <lq>There was movement at the station</lq>`
	`</p>`

tables within paragraphs	<p>Examples of content structures include: <simpletable> ... </simpletable> </p>
code blocks within paragraphs	<p>Client variables are set as in the example: <codeblock>Dim cli as String cli=43 </codeblock> </p>
lists within paragraphs	<p>There are two XRW variants: <sl> <li>XRW</li><li>XRW Super</li> </sl> </p>

Some content models may not permit nesting in this way, such as where both the blocks are `p` elements, but as an objective, this nesting approach should be preferred.

> **Note:** There are some conflicting requirements when the content needs to be localized. Including a block nested inside a paragraph, such as in the preceding examples, will create some problems for translators. This creates a dilemma which may eventually be solved by advancements in software tools. If you are writing for translation, you avoid including text after a nested block inside another block element. The guidelines contained in the *Best Practice for Leveraging Legacy Translation Memory when Migrating to DITA (Joseph & Raya, 2007)* whitepaper produced by the OASIS DITA Translation Subcommittee should be followed when writing for translation.

Paragraphs (and other block elements) within tables

In DITA, the cells of a table normally contain plain text (technically, *string data*). However, table cells may also contain paragraphs, lists, and other block elements (*block data*). This characteristic of table cells results in a choice for authors of whether to enter plain text or paragraphs in cells.

For example, a simple table cell could be coded as *string data* `<stentry>2.5 litre engine</stentry>` or *block data*

`<stentry><p>2.5 litre engine</p></stentry>`. It is also technically valid to have a mix of string and block data, where one cell has plain text and another has paragraphs.

The best practice mark-up is the simplest mark-up.

If there is just one block of text in the cell, then the cell should be left as *string data*. This stores the minimum of mark-up, and simplifies the processed output. If there are multiple blocks in the cell, then paragraphs (or other block items) should be used. *String data* should not be used in the same cell as *block data*.

If there is a need for one cell to include block elements, then all cells should be consistently treated. Using mixed mark-up methods (blocks in some cells and string-only in others) are likely to result in inconsistent rendering of the output.

In particular, simple tables (`simpletable` elements) should be kept as simple as possible. If a table requires block elements in cells, it should be coded as a normal table rather than a simple table.

Paragraphs (and other block elements) within notes

The `note` element can contain one or more paragraph (`p`) or other *block data* elements. Both `note` and `p` are block elements.

Mark-up options of:

```
<note>
 There are four forced induction models.
</note>
```

and

```
<note>
 <p>There are four forced induction models.</p>
</note>
```

are both valid, but using both mark-up options will result in inconsistency.

It is arguable that the two options are semantically different. A paragraph is a self-contained unit dealing with a single idea. A note has a separate semantic purpose, to highlight ancillary or associated ideas. A single note therefore has no need to contain a paragraph. However, in many cases, there will be more than one ancillary (note) idea, resulting in a need to break the note text into constituent blocks.

The simplest form of mark-up reflects the best practice.

If there is just one block of text in the note, then the note should be left as string-only. This stores the minimum of mark-up, and simplifies the processed output. If there are multiple blocks in the note, then paragraphs, lists (or other block elements) should be used. Never start with string data followed by a block.

In a set of notes, if there is a need for one note to include block elements, then all notes in the set should be consistently treated. Using mixed mark-up methods (blocks in some notes and string-only in others) are likely to result in inconsistent rendering of the output.

String-only text should not be used in the same note alongside block elements.

Paragraphs (and other block elements) within list items

If there is just one block of text in the list item, then that item should be left as plain text (*string data*). This stores the minimum of mark-up, and simplifies the processed output. If there are multiple blocks in the list item, then paragraphs (or other block items) should be used. *String data* text should not be used in the same list item alongside block elements.

Paragraphs in reference topics

Reference topics are designed to contain look-up information, typically organized in a tabular form. As such, paragraph elements containing more narrative ideas than look-up data will normally have no place in a reference topic.

The DITA standard does not permit `p` elements in the body of a reference topic unless contained within elements such as `refsyn` and `section`.

Do not use workarounds (such as embedding p elements in sections without titles) in order to include a paragraph. Avoid inserting multiple paragraphs in syntax descriptions (`refsyn` elements), as these elements are intended to be brief descriptions.

As with other information types, you should avoid using section elements wherever possible.

Poetry, dialog and fragments of text

The `lines` element may be used to represent character dialog, and text fragments where the line breaks can be considered to be part of the content. A good example of the `lines` element is to describe a poem.

A processor will treat line-end characters within a `lines` element to be part of the data; normally, for most other elements, line-end characters are ignored.

The `lines` element is similar to the `pre` element in HTML.

Identifying programming code

Examples of programming, scripting, or mark-up language code are marked up using the code phrase (`codeph`) and code block (`codeblock`) elements. As the element names suggest, code phrase is used when the code sample occurs inline within a paragraph or other block element, while code block is used when the code is more than one line long, and is a block in its own right.

Code block elements can be nested inside a paragraph (or other block element).

If you have text that introduces the codeblock and more text that immediately explains the code, you can use a structure such as in the following example:

```
<p>
  If you display debugging information, such as in:
  <codeblock>
    debugText = app.name & app.ver
    debug.print("Value is " & debugText)
  </codeblock>
  you must launch the application in debugging mode.
</p>
```

Line breaks can be used inside `codeblock` elements.

Procedures and steps

The purpose of procedural documents is to explain to the reader how to accomplish tasks. The task information type is specifically designed for procedures, with a well-defined structure built around steps.

Semantics in steps

Of the three original base information types in DITA, the task type is the most *strongly typed*. In other words, the task information type has the strictest rules. A task must be made up of one set of steps only. If you feel you need more than one set of `steps`, you almost certainly need to create more than one task topic.

In most cases, a set of steps is made up of one or more `step` elements, with each `step` element comprising a mandatory command (`cmd`) element, and an optional `stepresult` element.

The syntax of a typical set of steps is as in the following example:

```
<steps>
  <step>
    <cmd>Turn the key to the right.<cmd>
    <stepresult>The engine light will illuminate.</
stepresult>
  </step>
  <step>
    <cmd>Press the <uicontrol>Start</uicontrol>
button.</cmd>
  </step>
</steps>
```

In some cases, the complexity of a set of steps requires a more complex structure. Three more sophisticated elements can be used in such cases:

- `substeps`
- `choices`
- `choicetable`

Examples are often a good way of explaining a task, and the task information type allows one (optional) example of a step to be included (`stepxmp`) after any `cmd` element, and for one (optional) overall example to be included after the `steps` block.

Explanatory information to support a command can optionally be added after the `cmd` within a `step` through the `info` element.

Before the `steps` block, the context in which a task is performed can be described through a `context` element. If there are any pre-requisites or pre-conditions for a task to be performed, these can be described in the `prereq` element above the `steps` block.

After the `steps` block, any post-requisites can be described (using the `postreq` element), and the overall result of the task steps can be described in a `result` element.

The overall structure of a task topic is:

```
<task>
 <shortdesc>...</shortdesc>
 <taskbody>
  <prereq>...</prereq>
  <context>...</context>
  <steps>
  ...
  </steps>
  <result>...</result>
  <example>...</example>
  <postreq>...</postreq>
 </taskbody>
</task>
```

Separating procedures into granular steps

DITA task information types have a structure where each step is designed to contain one command only. This one command per step principle can be stretched a little, such as in the following example.

```
<step><cmd>Enter your password, and
click <uicontrol>OK</uicontrol>.</cmd></step>
```

In this example, there are technically two actions (entering the password, and clicking the OK button), but a simple action such as "clicking OK" can be treated as part of the entering text step.

However, aside from this exception, steps must be limited to one action or command. For example, the following is semantically incorrect (although technically *valid*).

```
<step><cmd>Browse to https://abc.com, and accept
the security certificate. Use factory defaults to
log in. (Enter user name <userinput>admin</
userinput>
and password <userinput>password</userinput>).</
cmd></step>
```

New DITA adopters often ask how a line break can be inserted into a `step` command. The answer is that it can't, because a line break is a formatting device, not a semantic device, and DITA only stores the semantics.

Restricting tasks to one procedures only

The task information type is specifically designed to contain one procedure only. If you feel you need to document two procedures in one task topic, you should re-examine your approach. Two procedures should be documented in two task topics.

If necessary, you can output two DITA task topics to one single output HTML topic, using the `chunk` attribute.

If you feel that you need to restart numbering within a task, then you probably have more than one procedure in the topic, and should split them into two separate task topics.

In some cases, what appears to be two procedures may turn out to be a nested procedure, in which case the `substeps` element can be used. The `choicetable` structure is also useful for procedures where a step has a number of alternative options.

If a procedure can be performed in two different ways, you should document those alternatives in two separate topics.

The `prereq` element

The optional pre-requisites (`prereq`) element in task topics is used to describe the things that a user needs to know or do before starting the task.

During output to a reading format, the pre-requisite (`prereq`) element should be labelled so that the reader can identify the information as being a pre-requisite state.

The `prereq` element must read as one or more complete sentences.

Normally you should only need to have one block of pre-requisite information, and you should not nest a single, redundant paragraph (`p`) element within the `prereq` element. However, if you need to include more than one block, you will need to nest paragraphs inside the `prereq` element.

For example, a typical single-block pre-requisite should be structured as:

```
<prereq>Ensure...</prereq>
```

while a lengthy pre-requisite with more than one block should be structured as:

```
<prereq>
  <p>Ensure...</p>
  <p>Prepare...</p>
</prereq>
```

If there are any topics that document pre-requisite tasks, these should be added as links in the `related-links` section at the bottom of the topic, with the `link` element's `importance` attribute set to required. This will result in those links being placed under the pre-requisites block during processing to a reading format.

The following example shows a typical presentation of a required link from the `related-links` section in a task topic processed to XHTML.

Figure 27: Typical XHTML output of `related-links` with `importance` setting of required

Configuring source addresses

The IP address (or range of IP addresses) to which a
Address tab of the Configuration window.

You must have been allocated a static IP address before co

Prerequisites
Applying for Static IP Address Allocation

Use the **Source Address** tab to specify the source IP addre

1. Click the **Source Address** tab.
2. Select one of the following settings:

Substeps within steps

In DITA, procedural steps can be structured in two levels: `steps` and `substeps`. Any step within a `steps` block can be broken down into `substeps`, but a `substep` cannot be further broken down.

If a procedural step is broken down into substeps, the `substeps` section can be used within an individual step (as a child of the `cmd` element). In other cases, a `choicetable` structure, designed for decision points in a step, may be appropriate.

The `substeps` element contains one or more `substep` elements, which are almost identical to the `step` element.

Avoid `substeps` whenever possible. If a step is a task in itself, it is best approach is to document that secondary task in a separate topic, and cross-reference the task topic to the second task topic. Your task should ideally be made up of a single level of steps. Re-writing a procedure is sometimes necessary to find a way of simplifying it to one level.

If you are documenting a procedure with two or more distinct variants, such as a procedure describing how to enable JavaScript in different browsers, you should create different task topics for each variant. For example, you would create one topic for "Enabling JavaScript in Internet Explorer", another for "Enabling JavaScript in Safari", and so on.

If the variation between procedures is only very slight, you may be able to write a single procedure but use `choices` or `choicetable` elements to distinguish the differences.

Single step procedure

A single step procedure should still be marked up using the `steps` structure, rather than `steps-unordered` or `steps-informal`.

Some writers object to the default processing of something like:

```
<steps>
       <step><cmd>Eject!</cmd></step>
<steps>
```

as

```
1. Eject!
```

because they feel the number is unwarranted or confusing.

However, the semantics of the DITA source should always be observed over any preference in output format. The output processing should be changed if the output needs to be different (in our case, represented as a bulleted item instead of a numbered item). The DITA source shouldn't be corrupted or "bent" to achieve a certain output result.

The command element

A step in a task is made up of a command (`cmd`) element, which is mandatory, and a number of optional elements such as `stepresult` and `stepxmp`.

The `cmd` element describes the action that the reader must take in order to complete the step.

Use active voice and the imperative mood in writing the command, and use only one, complete sentence. If you need to expand on the details of the command, use a sibling information (`info`) element. Do not include the system response or the result of the user performing the action; that information should be described in a sibling step result (`stepresult`) element.

Required and optional steps

The `step` and `substep` elements have an optional `importance` attribute, which has two valid values: optional and required. The attribute is used to indicate whether the step is optional (within a set of mandatory steps), or required (within a set of optional steps). The optional setting is more commonly used than required.

During processing to a reading format, steps with an `importance` attribute are typically rendered with an "Optional:" or "Required:" prefix.

Figure 28: Typical rendering of step with importance attribute set

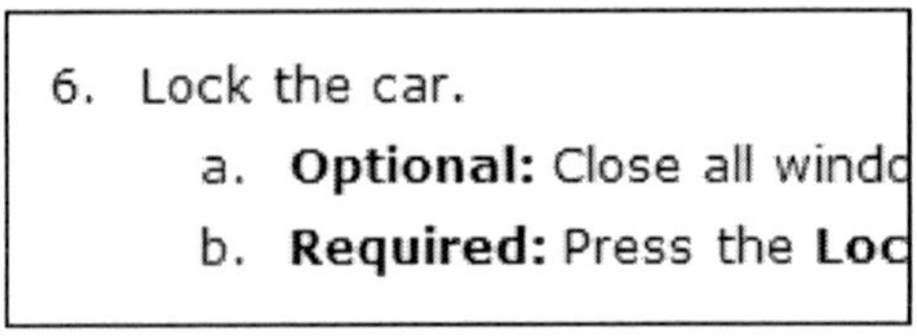

6. Lock the car.
    a. **Optional:** Close all windo
    b. **Required:** Press the **Loc**

Complex nested tasks

Tasks are sometimes differentiated into procedures and processes, where processes are high level overviews of a set of procedures, while procedures are detailed instructions for performing a task.

A process could be documented using a `task` information type, with each step of the process correlating to a procedure.

Figure 29: Structural relationship between process and procedures

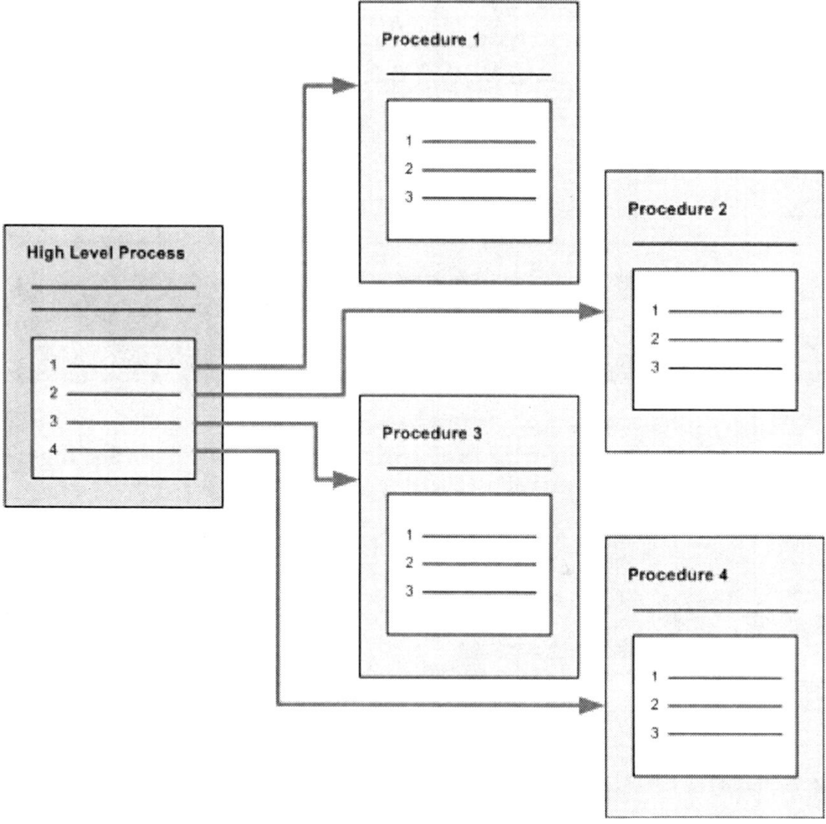

While it is possible to hyperlink the individual steps of the process to the corresponding procedure topic, this is not recommended. Nor is it recommended to provide a `related-links` section in the process topic to link to the related procedure topics.

Best practice is to leave the high level process topic as a *stub topic*, with minimal information in it (typically just a title and a short description).

The information type of the process topic should be either `concept` or `task`. The procedure topics should be arranged as child topics of the process topic in the ditamap, with the `collection-type` attribute of the process (parent) topic set to sequence. This arrangement will result in the process steps being automatically generated during processing, with the steps based on the titles of the child procedure topics. Any short descriptions in the procedure topics will also be included with the process steps. The sequence setting will result in the generated links being arranged in to a numbered list.

The *stub topic* approach to processes allows for much easier re-use, and removes re-keying of process steps. If one procedure is not used in a particular publishing scenario, the process topic won't need to be edited at all.

Figure 30: Example of a stub topic after processing

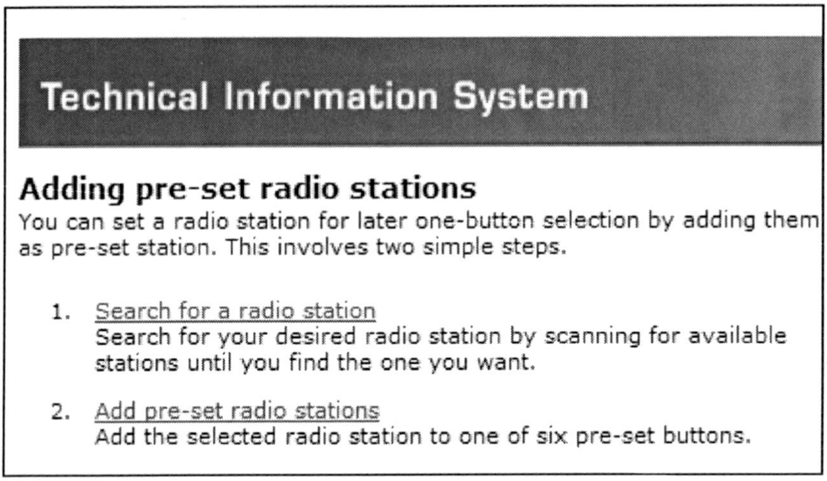

Notes and extra information in a step

A command (`cmd`) element in a task topic step cannot contain a `note` element. Extra information to help explain the step should be contained in an `info` element.

If the extra information is a warning, caution or otherwise requires special highlighting, you can place a `note` element within an `info` element.

The coding of a `note` within an `info` element is shown in the example:

```
<step>
  <cmd>Click <uicontrol>OK</uicontrol>.</cmd>
     <info>
             <note type="caution">Never enter your
password when connecting to an
                FTP site from within the corporate
firewall.</note>
  </info>
</step>
```

Figure 31: Typical rendered result of a caution `note` in an `info` element within a `step`

4. Click **OK**.
   CAUTION:
   Never enter your password when connecting to an F

> **Note:** For some documents, particularly for the machine industry, there are strict standards regarding the placement of *hazard statements* (warnings, cautions and other *admonishments*). Before DITA 1.2, it was not always possible to place warning statements to conform with the ANSI Z535 and ISO 3864-2 standards for hazard statements without specializing the `task` information type.
> DITA 1.2 introduced a new information type, `machineryTask`, which fully conforms with the requirements of ANSI Z535 and ISO 3864-2.

Images within steps

Images can be used to support documentation of task steps, as `image` elements within the `cmd` element, or as `image` elements within the `stepxmp` or `info` elements.

Figure 32: Task topic `steps` structure showing `image` within a `step`

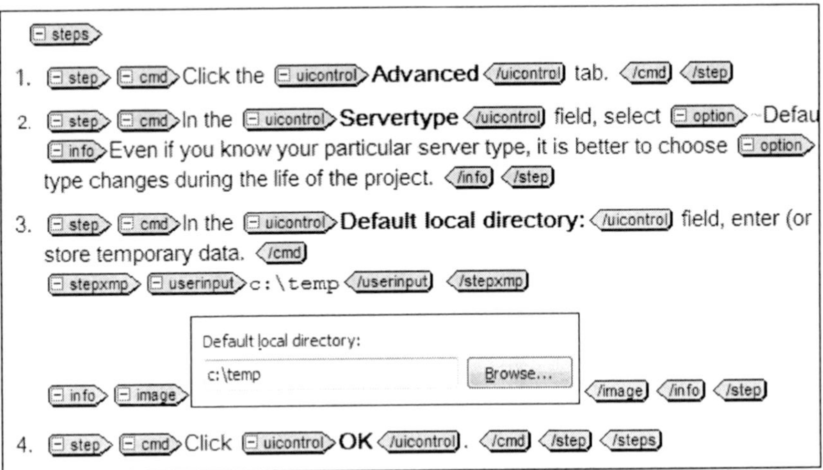

Figure 33: Typical rendered result of steps mark-up

1. Click the **Advanced** tab.
2. In the **Servertype** field, select `Default (Autodetect)`. Even if you know
   type changes during the life of the project.
3. In the **Default local directory:** field, enter (or browse for) the name of th
   Example: `c:\temp`

   Default local directory:
   c:\temp
   Browse...
4. Click **OK**.

Choice tables

The `choicetable` element is an extremely useful device for documenting options within a single step of a task.

As the name suggests, `choicetable` content is structured in a table, with one column for the option or choice, and another column for the description of the option or choice. If column headings are required, they can be specified through `choptionhd` and `chdeschd` elements within a `chhead` header row. A row within a choice table is defined with a `chrow` element containing an option (`choption`) element and a description (`chdesc`) element.

The recommended column headings are "Option" and "Description".

The structure of the choice table is shown in the code sample:

```
<choicetable>
  <chhead>
    <choptionhd>Option</choptionhd>
    <chdeschd>Description</chdeschd>
  </chhead>
  <chrow>
    <choption>Any</choption>
    <chdesc>Applies the rule to any IP address.</
chdesc>
  </chrow>
  <chrow>
    <choption>Single IP Address</choption>
    <chdesc>
      <p>Applies the rule to one IP address.</p>
      <note>Use the dotted decimal format. Example:
127.0.0.1</note>
    </chdesc>
  </chrow>
</choicetable>
```

Figure 34: Typical formatting of a `choicetable` in an output format

2. Select one of the following settings:

Option	Description
Any	Applies the rule to any IP address.
Single IP Address	Applies the rule to one IP address. **Note:** Use the dotted decimal format. Example: 127.0.0.1

Although more than one `choicetable` is permitted in a step, only one should be used.

The `choicetable` has a key column (`keycol`) attribute which nominates which column should be treated as row headings. For most publishing tools, a setting of `0` will result in all of the row content (except for the header row) displaying in Roman text, while a setting of `1` results in the first (choice) column content displaying in bold. Although not often appropriate, a setting of `2` will result in the second (description) column content typically displaying in bold.

The recommended `keycol` attribute setting for the `choicetable` element is `1`.

Non-sequential procedural steps

Until DITA 1.2, the base content model only offered steps as a semantic structure for procedures, processes and instructions. In many ways, this one-size-fits-all approach was very limiting. A `substeps` element provided some scope for more complex procedures, but some believed that an upper level `process` element was required.

DITA 1.2 introduced the `steps-informal` and the `steps-unordered` alternatives to `steps`. The `steps-informal` structure in only available in the *general task* information type, while `steps-unordered` can be used in the *(strict) task* and the *general task* information types. One of the reasons for the introduction of the new types of steps was to provide for processes.

The `steps-informal` structure should be used for documenting processes where there are no distinct steps or stages.

The `steps-unordered` structure should be used when there are distinct steps in the procedure or process, but the order in which they are performed is not important. In other words, use `steps-unordered` in the same way that you might use an unordered list (`ul`) in a concept topic.

Do not use `steps-informal` or `steps-unordered` as a lazy way of writing unstructured steps (that is, steps without the `cmd/stepresult/info` vocabulary).

If you feel you need non-sequential substeps in a `step` element, use the `choicetable` structure rather than `steps-informal`. There is no `substeps-informal` structure.

Tables

Types of tables

The two types of general purpose tables in base DITA are:

table The standard `table` structure is designed for complex, tabular information, where a title can be applied to the table. The `table` can also be easily cross-referenced, and a "List of Tables" generated during the publishing process.

simpletable The `simpletable` structure is a much simplified design, with no provision for titles or cross-referencing. It is used for informal, simple tabular information.

Both types of table are based on the CALS standard table structure; the table structure of HTML is based on the same standard.

DITA also includes some special purpose tables, including relationship tables (used in ditamaps for cross-reference metadata) and `properties` tables (used in reference topics).

Working with tables

The principle of the separation of content and form reaches a stumbling block when it comes to tabular information and tables. Tables are both a content structure and a presentational form construct. The content of a table is a set of data organized into rows with a common structure. The form of a table is its column and row widths, its borders, its padding, etc.

As a matter of principle, a DITA topic shouldn't be storing any information about how any content is presented. However, there is a need to specify some formatting information that is specific to an individual table, and that cannot be applied automatically during the publishing process. DITA does therefore include the capacity to store some formatting information alongside content in table elements. When content and form are bound together in this way, re-use of the content becomes more difficult. For example, if I specify that a table should be 25 cm wide, the topic containing the table can't be easily output to a page or column narrower than 25 cm.

For this reason, tables should be treated carefully. They should be avoided where there is no loss of meaning, they should never be used as a formatting device alone, and any unavoidable formatting information should be kept to a minimum.

DITA's table content model is based on the OASIS interchange form of *CALS* tables. It is not possible to create a table specialization with a footer based on the `thead` element, because the underlying content model specifies that a table can only have a `thead` then a `tbody`, and not two `thead` elements or two `tbody` elements.

The formatting elements and attributes within DITA table structures are:

- `colspec` (column specification) element (`tgroup`)
- `align` attribute (`colspec`, `tgroup`, `entry`)
- `char` (character alignment) attribute (`colspec`)
- `charoff` (character offset) attribute (`colspec`)
- `colsep` (column separator) attribute (`table`, `colspec`, `tgroup`, `entry`)
- `colwidth` (column width) attribute (`colspec`)
- `frame` attribute (`table`)
- `pgwide` (page wide placement) attribute (`table`)
- `rowsep` (row specification) attribute (`table`, `colspec`, `tgroup`, `row`, `entry`)
- `scale` attribute (`table`)
- `valign` (vertical alignment) attribute (`tbody`, `row`, `entry`)

In addition, there is a `rowheader` attribute (of the `table` element) that nominates whether the first rows contains heading information; this is arguably *content metadata* rather than *form*.

DITA does not support table footers.

The `keycol` and `refcols` attributes

The `choicetable`, `simpletable` and `properties` table elements have a `refcols` attribute and a `keycol` attribute.

The key column (`keycol`) attribute nominates which column in the table should be used for any row headings. For most publishing tools, a setting of `0` (no column is the key column) will result in all of the row content displaying in Roman text, while a setting of greater than zero will result in the corresponding column being displayed in bold (or otherwise highlighted). For example, a setting of `1` results in the first column content displaying in bold.

The cross-reference columns (refcols) attribute functions in a similar way to keycol attribute. It designates the number of the columns that contain references, with the intention that the contents of these columns will be automated linked during processing to an output format. Columns are identified by a space-delimited list of numbers. For example, a setting of 1 3 indicates that the first and third columns contain cross-reference information. The refcols attribute is not used by many, if any, publishing tools. However, it is provided in the DITA standard for possible future use.

Column and row headers

A column header row is specified through a thead row in the table. The thead element contains normal table cell (entry) elements.

If the first cell in each row is a heading (in other words, if the first column is a header column), you can specify this in the standard table by setting the rowheader attribute to firstcol. You cannot specify any other column to be the header column in a standard table.

With a simpletable, you can use the keycol attribute of the simpletable element to nominate the number of the column that contains the row headings. For example, setting the keycol attribute of the simpletable element to 1.

Nested tables

DITA supports nested tables (table and simpletable) through a small workaround. While the DITA content model does not allow a table cell (entry element) to include a table element, it does allow a p element. And a p element can contain a table.

A table can therefore be nested within a table cell provided a paragraph is first added. This results in the following structure:

```
<table>
 <tbody>
  <row>
   <entry>
     <p><table>....</table></p>
   </entry>
  ...
  </row>
```

```
 </tbody>
</table>
```

In the interests of simplicity, you should not use nested tables. Complex tables can often be avoided by chunking the information into smaller units.

If the type of information is such that nested tables are absolutely necessary, you should only include simple tables (`simpletable`) within other tables. In other words, you should use a `simpletable` within a (normal) `table`, or a `simpletable` within a `simpletable`, but not a (normal) `table` within a (normal) `table`. The more complex structure of normal tables (such as titles and column specifications) may cause processing problems. It is not semantically sound to include a full table structure within an existing full table structure.

Note: Some publishing tools cannot process nested tables.

Phrases

Program, script and routine names

The DITA programming domain is a set of mark-up elements used for documenting programming languages and their use. The software domain is a similar set of elements used for documenting software applications.

To identify a program or script name within an end-user's use of a software application, you should use the `cmdname` (command name) element (from the software domain).

To identify a function, API or sub-routine within documentation aimed at programmers, you should use the `apiname` (API name) element (from the programming domain).

Referring to a program name

```
<step><cmd>After resetting the
computer, run
the <cmdname>syscheck</cmdname>
program to verify
the recovery.</cmd></step>
```

Referring to a sub-routine or function

```
<p>You can link the <apiname>print</
apiname> sub-routine to
the button's <apiname>onclick</
apiname> event.</p>
```

Parameter and variable names

In computer science, a parameter is a type of variable which is passed to a program or sub-routine. The term *parameter* is closely associated with the term *argument*; a parameter is defined in the procedure definition itself, while the argument is the value passed to the procedure in the procedure call. (In this context, a *procedure* means a program function, routine or sub-routine.)

For example, in the `CalcCharge` procedure following, the arguments are hourlyRate and numHours..

```
Function CalcCharge(hourRate as Integer, numHours as
Integer) as Integer
  Return (hourRate * numHours)
End Function
```

When the `CalcCharge` procedure is called, the values passed to the procedure are the parameters; in this case, the values 55 and 130.

```
grossFee = CalcCharge(55,130)
```

In some cases, the values passed will be variables; that is, they will be a named substitute for the value.

```
hr = 55
co = 130
grossFee = CalcCharge(hr,co)
```

The three terms *parameter*, *argument*, and *variable* are often used interchangeably, to the point that their specific meanings are often confused. To further confuse matters, their meaning in documentation is subtly different. For example, a variable in documentation is a placeholder in the text that the reader needs to substitute with values particular to the reader.

DITA has four elements used for identifying parameters, arguments, and variables: `parmname` (parameter name), `parml` (parameter list), `varname` (variable name), and `var` (variable).

parm ...programming parameters and arguments ...calls, and functions. Documentation usually ...n the parameters (the information passed to a ...ure), rather than the procedure's arguments, so ...mname is appropriately named. The `parmname` element belongs to DITA's programming domain; it is intended for documenting APIs rather than applications.

...ml Used to identify a list of programming parameters and arguments in commands, calls, and functions. The parml element has a list structure, comprising `plentry` (row), `pt` (parameter term), and `pd` (parameter definition). The `parmname` element belongs to DITA's programming domain; it is intended for documenting APIs rather than applications.

varname Used when the reader has to substitute a value that might be specific to their own context or environment. For example, when documenting how to log on to a system, the user name (which will vary from user to user) will be marked up as `<varname>`. The `varname` element belongs to DITA's software domain; it is intended for documenting software applications.

var Used only in syntax diagrams (`syntaxdiagram`), which are special devices used to document programming languages, and *application programming interfaces (APIs).* The `var` element belongs to DITA's programming domain; it is intended for documenting programming environments.

When documenting the example `CalcCharge` function, the following approach might be used.

```
<p>The <apiname>CalcCharge</apiname> has two
parameters:
 <parml>
   <plentry>
    <pd>rate</pd>
    <pt>The hourly rate charged to the client.</pt>
   </plentry>
   <plentry>
    <pd>hours</pd>
```

```
    <pt>The total number of hours spent on the
client's project.</pt>
   </plentry>
 </parml>
</p>
<p>Both <parmname>rate</parmname> and
<parmname>hours</parmname> must be integer values.
</p>
```

By contrast, the `varname` element might be used in a description of a Vehicle Identification Number in a car owner's manual as:

```
<p>The VIN number has the following structure:
 <varname>Place of Manufacture</varname>
 <varname>Model</varname>
 <varname>Make</varname>
 <varname>Engine</varname>
 <varname>Type</varname>
 <varname>Equipment</varname>
 <varname>Check Digit</varname>
 <varname>Year of Manufacture</varname>
 <varname>Production Number</varname>
</p>
```

In a software user guide, the `varname` element might be used when describing a directory location, as in:

```
<p>The transfer file is generated by the
<cmdname>Build</cmdname> application into the
<filepath><varname>My Documents</varname>\acme\xfer</
filepath> folder.</p>
```

In summary, use `parmname` for programming variables, parameters, and arguments, and `varname` for other documentation variable placeholders.

Do not use square brackets or other syntactical conventions for simple variable names. If your publishing tool does not insert those conventions during processing, you may need to configure the tool so that it does so.

Messages displayed in a user interface

Whether it is through a software application, a machine instrument panel, or a consumer electronic device display, information is commonly displayed to the user through some sort of user interface. In some cases the information takes the form of lights, gauges, and dials, in other cases the information is audible, and in other cases it is textual or graphical. When describing these messages from the equipment in DITA, a number of semantic elements are used.

The main message elements are:

msgph A short textual message displayed on a screen, as a sound, or on a printout. This element is used when the message will be described or quoted within an existing paragraph or block element.

msgblock A long, multi-line textual message displayed on a screen, as a sound, or on a printout. This element is used when the message will be described or quoted in its own block element (or paragraph).

msgnum The identification number of a message, such as an error message, usually displayed on a screen or instrument panel, or on a printout.

systemoutput The response from a system to user input of some kind. This element is part of the DITA software domain.

Error messages are usually made up of a `msgnum` element (the error code) and a `msgph` or `msgblock` element. Likewise, status messages are best described with `msgph` or `msgblock`. The resulted displayed on a calculator after a user has entered an equation is best described with a `systemoutput` element.

The distinction between a message and system output is that the message is something produced by the system or device as part of its function, while a system output is something that the system returns as a direct result of something that the user inputs. Another way of putting it is that the `systemoutput` is used in conjunction with `userinput` to describe a "conversation" between the user and the system.

Printouts, read-outs and other system output

The system output (`systemoutput`) element is used to describe the display or read-out from the device, application or system being documented. The `systemoutput` element is similar to the `msgph` element in that both elements describe the output from a system. The `msgph` element specifically describes a system message; `systemoutput` is less specific.

The `systemoutput` element should also be used when describing snippets of text from a printout from a computer application or system, such as words on the printed page.

Example:

```
<p>Second and subsequent level numbers in a nested
ordered
list are typically rendered following the format of
<systemoutput>1. a. I.</systemoutput>.</p>
```

Trademarks and service marks

A trademark is a distinctive word, phrase, sign, symbol or other indicator used by an organization to identify its products or services, or the organization itself. Trademark laws vary from country to country, although there are international conventions including the Trademark Law Treaty, the Madrid System of registering trademarks in multiple jurisdictions, and *World Trade organization* agreements.

DITA includes a trademark (`tm`) element to identify trademark words or phrases. However, there is specific provision for identifying images as trademarks.

The `tm` element has a required `tmtype` attribute, which has three valid values:

reg registered trademark

tm unregistered trademark

sm service mark (not widely used outside USA)

When processed to an output format, the value of the `tmtype` attribute will typically be used to apply the applicable standard symbol to the trademark or service mark, such as ® or ™.

The `tm` element also has an optional `tmclass` attribute, which can be used for different classifications of reg, tm, and sm. More importantly, the `tm` element has `trademark` and `tmowner` attribute. The `trademark` attribute is used when the content of the `tm` element is different to the legal trademark itself. The `tmowner` attribute is used to identify the name of the legal entity that owns the trademark.

Without any special provision for identifying the trademark detail of an image, a workaround is to code the trademark inside a `term` element inside the alternative text (alt element) value for the image, as in the example:

```
<image href="...">
 <alt>
  <term>
   <tm tmtype="reg" tmowner="IBM Corp.">IBM</tm>
  </term>
 Logo</alt>
</image>
```

Keyboard keystrokes

It is not immediately obvious in DITA which element should be used to mark up keyboard keys, such as **Enter**, **Ctrl** and **Backspace**. The best approach (without resorting to specialization) is to use the uicontrol and userinput elements, depending on context.

When describing keys on a computer keyboard, use the uicontrol element. For example, `<p>Use the <uicontrol>Tab<uicontrol> to move from field to field.</p>`.

> **Note:** Do not use the shortcut element; this element is for identifying keyboard shortcuts in descriptions of user interface controls in windowed applications.

When describing a series of keystrokes, or data, that the user must input, use the userinput element. For example, `<cmd>Enter <userinput>1234</userinput>, then <uicontrol>Tab</uicontrol> to continue.</cmd>`.

Do not bracket the key name, such as by using square brackets around "Tab" to form `<uicontrol>[Tab]</uicontrol>`.

If the keyboard keys or keystrokes need to be rendered differently from other user interface controls (such as fields and buttons) in the output, then a specialization should be created. An alternative is to use a consistent outputclass attribute on the keyboard elements.

Footnotes

A footnote is usually seen as being specific to page layout output formats, so marking up text as a footnote could be viewed as recording presentational information within content; something that DITA tries to avoid.

However, footnotes can also be considered as semantic identifiers for supplementary information that doesn't belong inline in the text. The footnote content is not critical to understanding the content, but provides extra information that may be useful to some readers.

The footnote (`fn`) element is typically rendered in the output as a number in the flow of the text and the footnote content at the bottom of the page or topic. The footnote number is automatically calculated during the publishing process. In hypertext output formats, the inline footnote reference number may be hyperlinked to the footnote at the bottom of the topic. Some publishing tools may display the footnote content in a popup window (in some hypertext output formats).

An example of a footnote (`fn`) element is:

```
<p>Always wear a seatbelt.
  <fn>Some jurisdictions allow a medical exemption
from wearing a seat belt
  in exceptional circumstances.</fn>
</p>
```

The `coderef` element

The `coderef` element, introduced in DITA 1.2, is a reference element like `xref` and `conref`. Its purpose is to allow the transclusion of XML and other blocks of code from an external file.

For example, you may want to include a sample block of HTML code stored in its own HTML file. When the `coderef` is processed, the referenced code file is imported, *escaped* (to convert the tagging delimiting characters such as "<" are displayed, rather than treated as DITA instructions), and then output in the same way as a static `codeblock` element.

The text element

The `text` element, introduced in DITA 1.2, identifies a snippet of plain text that has no other special meaning (or presentation requirement). It should only be used when no other semantic element is appropriate. The text element is almost identical to the `ph` element, but cannot contain nested semantic element in the way that `ph` can contain, for example, `image` elements.

At first look, there seems to be no reason for having an element to contain text that has no semantic meaning! However, there are special circumstances when the `text` element makes sense, and that's when some text needs to be distinguished from other text, and when no other elements are allowed. The most likely example of this is when some text needs to be transcluded with a *conref* into a place where other elements are not permitted.

Do not use `text` in a place where `ph` is valid.

Product, company names, and other keywords

When used inline within the body content, a `keyword` element identifies names that have a special meaning, such as company names, product names, project names, department names, and categories.

These sort of names are almost always repeated in a suite of documents, so you should endeavor to re-use `keyword` elements using the conref feature.

The `keyword` element is not related to the `kwd` element, which is used in syntax diagrams to identify programming keywords.

Complex command reference content

In style-based authoring, formatting conventions have been used to identify the parts of command syntax for computer software applications. In this context, a command is a string of text that a user types in order to run an application and pass arguments to the application.

The *Microsoft Manual of Style for Technical Publications* suggests a syntax of:

- command in bold
- a set of choices surrounded by { }
- individual choices separated by |
- variable names in italics

- repeatable arguments indicated by ...
- optional items surrounded by [ ] or [[ ]].

For example, a command syntax might be represented as **ant** [-f *filename*] [-logfile *filename*] [-verbose].

In DITA, the following semantic elements are used to identify the components of a command:

kwd A literal keyword used in a command, utility or batch file

option an option or switch that modifies a command

oper An operator (such as *, + or =)

var The name of a variable or argument

delim A delimiter character used to identify the beginning or end of one part of the syntax

sep A separator character such as a bracket that is used within syntax

The syntax mark-up should be contained as a whole within a syntax phrase (`synph`) or syntax block (`synblk`) element.

An example of a marked up command line might be:

```
<synph>
 <kwd>ant</kwd> <option>-f</option> <var>filename</
var>
 <option>-logfile</option> <var>filename</var>
 <option>-verbose</option>
</synph>
```

A typical output of this code is:

`ant -f` *`filename`* `-logfile` *`filename`* `-verbose`

When the command syntax is being used within an instruction to a user (usually within a task topic), the syntax should instead be contained within a `userinput` element, without the individual components of the command semantically identified.

Marking up mark-up languages

When documenting XML mark-up languages, you should use the syntax phrase (synph) element to identify the names of language elements and attributes.

Do not use angular brackets to identify names of elements, or prefix attribute names with "@". These formatting conventions should be added, if required, during the publishing process.

You should consider specializing `synph` into two separate elements, one to identify elements and one to identify attributes, to better semantically differentiate the two.

If you are including code snippets rather than describing the name of an element or attribute, use the code phrase (`codeph`) or code block (`codeblock`) element, and not the `synph` element.

Phrases in different languages

Words or phrases in different human languages, dialects or spelling conventions can be identified through a phrase (`ph`) element with the `xml:lang` attribute storing the name of the language in the IETF BCP 47 and ISO 639 standard conventions.

If these words or phrases have a particular semantic meaning, such as a term expressed in a foreign language, then the mark-up element used should have its `xml:lang` attribute set to the foreign language.

For example, if the term *schadenfreude* is used within an English language topic, the mark-up would be:

```
<p>
  He experienced a sense of <term
xml:lang="de">schadenfreude</term>
</p>
```

Special characters and dates

Special characters and dates require different handling than normal text.

Non-breaking spaces and special characters

Your authoring tool may allow the insertion of non-breaking spaces between words. Non-breaking spaces are intended for use when the separation of two adjacent words through line wrapping will result in a loss of meaning or legibility. For example, some authors prefer values and their units, such as “12 kg”, to be treated as a single word.

Likewise, soft hyphens are intended for use when there is a preferred point for the breaking of a word during line wrapping.

Some mark-up languages support *entities*, which allow special characters (not included in the standard character set or not associated with keyboard keys) to be defined using a memorable shortcut. For example, HTML has a ` ` entity for non-breaking spaces. Regardless, provided a character is included in the relevant Unicode character set, it can be included in XML-based content using hexadecimal *numeric character references*, or *character escapes*.

Although XML supports entities, the DITA standard itself does not define any text entities. Nonetheless, character escapes can be used. The character escapes for commonly used special characters is:

non-breaking space	` `
soft hyphen	``
micro symbol	`µ`
non-breaking space	` `
division symbol	`ɇ`
en dash	`–`
em dash	`—`
ellipsis	`…`

Dates

There is no semantic element in DITA for dates in the flow of text in content, and they are therefore simply typed into the content.

You should, however, use consistent and standard notations for dates. Dates are represented numerically in different ways in different cultures, even within the same language group. Interational Standard ISO 8601 specifies rules for the numeric representation of dates; you should follow these standards where possible.

Chapter 4: Language and punctuation

What's in this chapter?

- Avoiding writing for output
- Stem sentences, glue text, and other transitional information
- Punctuation in lists
- Titles and headings
- Crafting paragraphs
- Different languages
- Quotation marks

> If language is not correct, then what is said is not what is meant; if what is said is not what is meant, then what must be done remains undone; if this remains undone, morals and art will deteriorate; if justice goes astray, the people will stand about in helpless confusion. Hence there must be no arbitrariness in what is said. This matters above everything.
>
> **Confucius**

Avoiding writing for output

If you find that you are deliberately coding your DITA topics in such a way as to achieve a particular output effect, you are without doubt taking the wrong path. DITA topics must be delivery-agnostic; they must be free of as much context (how the information is going to be used, presented or sequenced) as possible.

Stem sentences, glue text, and other transitional information

Transitional information, or *glue text*, is text used to inform readers of what has come before and what will follow later. In other words, it leads the reader from one idea to the next idea. When working in a modular documentation system, the author cannot assume what will come before or after, because information chunks can be assembled in different sequences and combinations to form different publications.

Some common forms of transitional information are found in:

- *stub content*, such as "In this chapter..."
- *stem sentences*, such as "To change the wheel:"
- *transitional phrases* , such as "Before starting, make sure you have..."
- cross-references, such as "For more information, see..."
- locational markers, such as "Next, we will describe..." and "Having completed the previous..."

In DITA, devices other than transitional text are used to maintain cohesion and to manage transition.

- Smaller information chunks, labelled with meaningful titles, reduce the need for stem sentences, particularly in task topics.
- Information typing separates content that may otherwise have been bundled together into distinct topics, thus breaking up generalist topics into, for example, concept, task and reference topics. This separation reduces the need for transitional text within topics.
- Using a structure where much of the context of a document is defined in the ditamap, rather than the topic, and the careful use of well-crafted short descriptions, allows stub content and cross-reference information to be automatically generated during the publishing process. For example, a `prereq` semantic element in a topic can be differentiated from other content by the application of labels or icons during the publishing process, and relationship tables can be used to form the links to related topics in the output.
- Adopting a minimalist approach to writing can also serve to eliminate superfluous transitional information.

In summary, avoid using transitional text, and rely on structure, meaningful titles and short descriptions, the separation of document context into the ditamap, and the publishing process, to achieve coherence, cohesion and transition.

Transitional information in semantic blocks

Transitional text in elements such as pre-requisites (`prereq`), context statements (`context`), results (`result`), and post-requisites (`postreq`) should be omitted.

There are a number of ways in which transitional text is incorrectly included in semantic blocks, such as in the following examples:

- "In this topic..." (within `shortdesc`)
- "The system must meet the following conditions before starting the procedure..." (within `context`)
- "Before entering the PIN you must complete some important checks..." (within `prereq`)
- "After completing the procedure you will find..." (within `postreq`)
- "In this procedure, the steps for..." (within `context`)

In DITA, alternative devices and a minimalist approach are used in place of transitional text. These devices include a publishing process that can systematically apply labels to parts of the output. For example, the words "Before you begin" and a graphical icon can be rendered in the output immediately before every pre-requisite `prereq` element text. Such systematic and consistent labelling allows semantic elements to be easily identified by the reader.

If your publishing process treats semantic elements such as `postreq` in the same way as normal paragraph (`p`) elements, you should change your publishing process to generate transitional information rather than change your writing approach to introduce redundant transitional information in your content.

Do not include labels, such as "Note", within the text of admonishment elements. The appropriate label or formatting will be applied when the paragraph is rendered during publishing.

Stem sentences in task topics

The DITA *task* information task doesn't have a dedicated element for a stem sentence to introduce the steps. The assumption that can be drawn is that a stem sentence (eg, "To change the wheel, proceed as follows") is not required. A descriptive topic title will obviate the need for a stem sentence, particularly when used in conjunction with a carefully crafted short description.

Do not break the semantics of your content by trying to force a stem sentence into a structure where it is not clearly permitted. For example, do not include a stem sentence as the last paragraph in the `context` element, using the logic that it will be rendered immediately before the step block.

The DITA Technical Committee did not forget to include a stem sentence element. It was deliberately not included, after careful consideration and consensus amongst the committee members.

Punctuation in lists

Punctuation in lists is already a contentious issue, but content re-use with conditional publishing in DITA makes it a little more so.

Punctuation options for ordered and unordered lists include:

- comma terminators for all items except the last, which has a full stop
- semicolon terminators for all items except the last, which has a full stop
- no terminators except for the last, which has a full stop

Some conventions include the word "and" at the end of the second last item.

Writing in a DITA environment, the context is removed from the content. This means that a list in the DITA source may not appear in the same sequence in the output. Some items might be removed by conditional publishing; for example, items relating to the administrator audience might be omitted from an output intended for novice users.

Because the second last item and the last item cannot be always identified, it is counter-productive to add "and" or different punctuation (eg, a full stop) at that point. (In other words, the second last and last items can't be treated as exceptions.)

List items should therefore have no closing punctuation, to maximize re-usability. An exception to this guideline is in the case of a list where all items are complete sentences.

In other cases, if considered necessary, a full stop can be added to the end of a list by the publishing process. For this approach to work, it is vital that **all** lists, including those with complete sentences, have no terminators.

Titles and headings

A title is not the same as a heading. A title is usually considered part of the content (and is typically rendered in the output as a heading), but it also has a role as a metadata container. For example, the title might be used as the basis for link text, outside the context of its topic. In that context, mark-up such as a footnote (`fn`) or cross-reference (`xref`) wouldn't make any sense.

A number of mark-up structures in DITA have titles, including:

- map
- topic
- table
- data
- link list
- syntax diagram
- figure
- section
- example

Avoid using phrase-level mark-up in titles, particularly when the motivation is to achieve a presentational outcome. For example, do not use footnote (`fn`) elements in titles, as the presentational outcome when a title is displayed in a pop-up window is likely to be unpredictable.

If a `title` element does not permit a particular type of phrase-level element, do not devise workarounds to force such elements in place.

For example, `title` does not permit the `cite` element, but does permit the general phrase (`ph`) element. That phrase element can itself contain `cite`. So while the code `<title>Such is Life <ph><cite>Ned Kelly</cite></ph></title>` is technically correct, it nonetheless constitutes a workaround, and should not be used.

Case in titles

It is possible to create titles for topics, figures and tables with letter case structures including the following:

- start case (first letter of each word capitalized, with the remainder lower case)
- all capitals
- title case (first letter of the first and last words capitalized, nouns and verbs initial capitalized, with the remainder lower case)
- all lower case
- all lower case except the first letter
- sentence case (first word and proper nouns initial capitalized, with the remainder lower case)
- camel case (the first letter of each word capitalized, with spaces and punctuation removed)

Other variations are also possible, such as "all lower case except nouns".

For titles in publications, the following options are the most common:

- all capitals
- title case
- sentence case
- all lower case

Title case and sentence case afford the maximum re-use possibilities, because they can be easily transformed, in the processing stage, into:

- start case
- all capitals
- all lower case
- camel case

You should use sentence case for all titles in DITA, other than publication titles. Sentence case is easier for an author to use, as it has simpler rules (first word and proper nouns must be initial capitalized).

The preceding applies to English, and may not be applicable in other languages (and writing systems) such as German, for example, where the first letter of all nouns is capitalized.

Line breaks in titles

Line breaks are formatting constructs, so in general, DITA mark-up doesn't provide for them. However, it's not quite so clear cut. Despite working to the ideal that content should be separated from form, DITA does provide for a good deal of form mark-up.

Table column widths can be specified in DITA, even though that's form. Image sizes can be specified in DITA, and that too is form.

It is possible to use these loopholes in the separation of content and form to make possible things such as line breaks in titles. For example, a workaround is to place a one pixel by one pixel image within the title, and set the image element's placement attribute to break. This will cause, in most outputs, the title to be displayed with text before the image displayed on a different line to text following.

You must avoid the temptation to use such workarounds in an attempt to introduce form into DITA content.

Where topic titles are used

Topic titles are extremely important in DITA, as they are used as both as a core navigation aid and for information labelling. The topic title can be generated in the output:

- as a heading in page layout output
- as a topic heading in Help and Web output
- as the page (and window) title in Help and Web output
- as hyperlink text in links automatically generated from ditamap hierarchies and relationship tables
- as text in cross-references
- as a Table of Contents entry
- as an Index entry
- as link text generated by a search engine
- in Dublin Core metadata in Help and Web content

Figure 35: DITA `title` elements are used in many places in a typical Help output

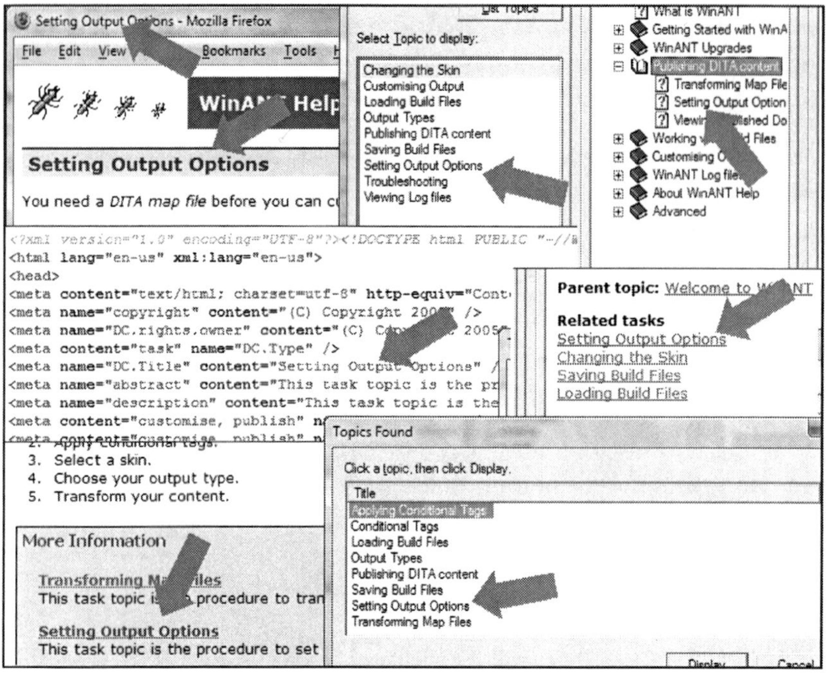

Crafting meaningful topic titles

In topic-based authoring, chunks of information have a greater need to be self-supporting, or standalone. This means that topics should be able to be read on their own, without reliance on what comes before or after. A topic with a heading of "Introduction" cannot be standalone, because it doesn't adequately describe what the topic is about. "Introducing the Supara Liberty" is a better label.

The greater importance of titles in semantic, structured authoring environments means that labeling (and other forms of cataloging) needs to be thorough, and time and skill must be devoted to crafting meaningful titles.

In addition to helping the reader understand what a topic is about, titles should also help the reader identify what kind of topic it is. From the topic title, readers should know whether the topic will help them understand something, help them do something, or provide supporting information. This can be done by using different phrasing for titles for topics of different information types.

Titles must be meaningful, easy to read, accurate, concise and consistent.

When composing titles, try constructing them as sentence fragments. A useful technique is to re-write the title after the content of the topic and the short description are complete.

Some more specific guidelines are:

- Do not use definite (eg, "the") and indefinite (eg, "an") articles ("Engine", not "The engine").
- Use the singular, not plural ("Engine", not "Engines").
- Do not start titles with generalized phrases ("Security" and "Maintenance", not "About security" and "Introduction to maintenance").
- Do not use the ampersand character ("Controls and switches", not "Controls & switches").
- Prefer the present participle (*-ing* form) verb and the imperative to the infinitive ("Starting the engine" or "Start the engine", not "To Start the Engine").
- Do not attempt to use line breaks.
- Use plain language.
- Aim to use no more than eight words.
- Use sentence case.
- Use qualitative words to make the title more specific ("reducing report length", not "report length", or "advantages of forced induction engines", not "forced induction").
- Ensure that the titles can be understood out of context.
- Use consistent syntax and parallel construction.

To help the reader identify the information type by the title, use the following guidelines.

Information Type	Syntax	Examples
Concept	Start with a noun or adjective	"Client window", "Supara Liberty features", "Important Considerations for Engine Modifications"
Task	Start with a gerund or present participle, and use singular nouns	"Resetting the odometer", "Printing the audit report"
Reference	Start with a noun or adjective, and include the reference construct (eg, "table", "list", etc)	"Specification table", "Product code list"

Conditional titles

Filtering `title` elements during publishing is risky, because `title` is sometimes a required element. Topic titles are a good example; a topic must always have a `title` element. Removing a topic's `title` element during publishing would result in invalid DITA, and the processing would inevitably fail. For this reason, the title element doesn't have `audience`, `platform`, `product` and `otherprops` attributes.

If it is necessary to apply conditions to parts of a title, you can mark up the `title` element text with phrase (`ph`) elements, and apply condition attributes to that element.

Crafting paragraphs

A paragraph should start with a *topic sentence*. A topic sentence establishes the paragraph's main idea, and therefore discloses the subject of the paragraph to the reader. This structure help scanning readers move quickly through a text.

The sentences that follow should support the topic sentence by elaborating on the main point. Paragraphs should be three to eight sentences in length.

To avoid closing off opportunities for re-using paragraphs in different contexts, do not use cohesive or transitional devices at the end of a paragraph that tie it to the next paragraph.

Different languages

It is not unusual to have content in more than one language in the same deliverable document, or even in the same topic. For example, a topic in German documenting a software application with a user interface in English might need to explain English language error messages.

Every DITA element, including `map` elements, topic elements, block elements and phrase elements, has an `xml:lang` attribute which stores the ISO 639 code of the human language in which the content is written.

If one topic has a mix of varieties or dialects of the same language, such as some US English and some UK English, the varieties can be managed through the `xml:lang` attribute.

For example, if the bulk of a concept topic's content was in US English, but one phrase was in UK English, the concept element's xml:lang attribute should be set to en-US, and the phrase marked up with `ph` or text with the `xml:lang` attribute set to en-UK.

If you need to deliver entire documents in different varieties or dialects of the same language, where there are significant spelling, punctuation and grammatical differences, you should treat the varieties as separate languages and manage the task as a localization project.

Quotation marks

Quotation marks are formatting constructs. They are arguably not punctuation, but highlighting devices like bold and italics. (In fact, in some cases, bold or italic is used in place of quotation marks.) However, they do contribute to the communication of meaning, in that they often indicate semantics.

Most commonly, quotation marks indicate that the encapsulated text is a literal quotation. DITA has `q` and `lq` elements (quotation and long quotation, respectively) which should be used to mark up the semantic meaning of "quotation". When the content is processed into a reading format, the rendering process may highlight the quoted text with italics, single quotation marks, double quotation marks, or any other available highlighting device. Or it may leave the quoted text unadorned. Your role as an author is simply to semantically identify quotations.

Other common uses of quotation marks are for highlighting purposes only, or for purposes more difficult to semantically identify. For example, quotation marks may be used to highlight the use of a new term (**this is what is known as "WYSIOO"**), to indicate a foreign term (**they preferred the "status quo"**) to indicate irony (**his autobiography is a great "novel"**), to cite a newspaper or reference (**it was in "The Age"**) or to reference popular culture (**that sausage was "noice"**).

If the DITA information type you are using does not provide a semantic element, you should try to re-phrase the text so that it reads unambiguously without the quotation marks.

In the *Cambridge Guide to Australian English Usage*, author Pam Peters points out that "ideally, the intended emphasis or meaning is conveyed by the choice of words, appropriately arranged". For example, prefixing the word "so-called" may help convey the meaning of irony or emphasis.

Malcolm Parkes, author of *Pause and Effect: An Introduction to the History of Punctuation in the West*, wrote of the quotation mark:

> Its primary function is to resolve structural uncertainties in a text, and to signal nuances of semantic significance which might otherwise not be conveyed at all, or would at best be much more difficult for a reader to figure out.
>
> **Parkes 1993**

According to Parkes, "quotation marks were gradually accepted during the first half of the eighteenth century", which certainly means that Shakespeare managed without them at all!

Nested quotations

Some complex quotations may include a quoted phrase within a quoted block, or less commonly, a quoted block within another quoted block.

In the first instance, a `q` element would be used within the `lq` block, and the processor would determine how quotation marks might appear in the output (typically, single quotes within double quotes).

An `lq` element can contain multiple paragraph (`p`) and other block elements.

The DITA standard does not permit an `lq` to nest directly inside another `lq` element, but it does permit a nested `lq` provided it is contained within a block element such as a `fig`. However, do not use this "loophole" to circumvent the disallowance of nested `lq` elements unless the use of the containing element is semantically correct.

In other words, the following:

```
<p>May read the description of John's speech at
Sanjay's wedding.</p>
 <lq>He rose from his seat and stood to his full
height.
  <fig>
   <lq>I have known the groom for most of his
life... I propose a toast to the groom.</lq>
  </fig>
  When he finished talking, he spilled his wine.
 </lq>
</p>
```

might be valid DITA, but it is not semantically correct DITA, because the contents of `fig` is not a figure.

Try to find a way of restructuring the text so that nested long quotations are not required.

Chapter 5: Graphics and figures

What's in this chapter?

- Figures and images
- Image file formats
- Image alignment, placement, and sizing
- Images in titles
- Callouts
- Localizing graphics
- Multimedia in DITA topics
- Figures containing tables
- Image maps
- WAI compliance

> Un bon croquis vaut mieux qu'un long discours. (A good sketch is better than a long speech.)
>
> **Napoléon Bonaparte**

Figures and images

Although images can be placed in a DITA topic as `image` elements without a surrounding `figure` element, figures are generally the best way to structure graphics and other illustrations. The exception is for simple inline images (that is, images that are part of the flow of the text), where an independent `image` element should be used.

Most commonly, images are stored is separate files external to DITA, but it is possible to embed XML-based image formats, such as *SVG*, within the DITA topic XML.

Figures in DITA are container elements typically comprising a `title` element, an `image` element, and a `desc` element.

The following example shows the DITA code for a typical figure.

```
<fig>
 <title>Charles Darwin</title>
 <desc>
  <cite>Photo: Library of Congress, Prints &
Photographs
  Division, [reproduction number, LC-USZ61-104]</
cite>
 </desc>
 <image placement="inline" align="right"
width="208px" height="320px"
  href="../images/darwin_library_of_congress.jpg">
  <alt>Photo of Charles Darwin: Library of Congress,
Prints and
  Photographs Division, [reproduction number, LC-
USZ61-104]</alt>
 <image>
</fig>
```

The `title` element contains a short, descriptive title of the figure. The `image` element's attributes contains the location, dimensions and placement of the image file, and a child `alt` element containing an alternative text description of the image (for reading devices that don't display images or readers who don't see images). The `desc` element contains further information about the image, including any photo credits or citations.

Although the `title` element appears before the `img` element in DITA mark-up, the sequence can be altered in the output by modifying the publishing process. Do not break the semantics by using workarounds (such as moving the `title` to `figgroup` element after the `img`) to achieve a formatting outcome.

The sample figure DITA code might result in the following when transformed into XHTML.

Figure 36: Example of a figure rendered in XHTML

of *On the Origin of Species*. DITA incorporates p
Darwinian theory (only in a completely different

Figure 1. Charles Darwin.
Photo: Library of Congress, Prints & Photographs Division, [r

Information Type refers to the focus on catego

Image file formats

DITA supports a variety of image formats. A more accurate assertion is that you can place a reference to any sort of image file inside a DITA `image` element, and it will be up to the publishing processor as to whether this image can be handled and generated into a reading format.

Typical image file types supported by current DITA processors include:

GIF	Compuserve Graphics Interchange Format
JPG	Joint Photographic Experts Group format
BMP	Microsoft Bitmap Picture format

TIF (or TIFF)	Tagged Image File Format
PNG	Portable Network Graphics format
EPS	Encapsulated PostScript format
SVG	*Scalable Vector Graphics* XML format

Unless you have specific reasons for choosing other formats, you should use SVG for line drawings and diagrams. Likewise, for photographs, use JPG with zero or low compression, particularly if you will be publishing to print formats. For other purposes, you should prefer PNG. If your publishing process does not support SVG, you may have to use PNG instead. However, a better approach is to use a publishing process which supports SVG.

> **Note:** These recommendations on image file types may not apply for specific publishing scenarios. For example, if you are using DITA to publish to high quality print, the TIFF format may be the best choice.

Image file management

Although there is no technical reason for taking this approach, you should store image files in a separate folder from content topics, for ease of organization and file management. Use a consistent folder name for images, typically `/images`.

Image files should be re-used as required in different topics across your content repository. Simplistically, image file re-use can be a matter of referencing the same image file. An example of this type of re-use is:

```
<concept>
...
<img href="../images/ej25.png" width="480px"
height="360px" />
...
</concept>

<task>
...
<img href="../images/ej25.png"  width="480px"
height="360px" />
...
</task>
```

Like other DITA elements, image elements can be re-used through conref transclusion. An alternative method to simplistic re-use of image files is to re-use `image` elements by conref, as in the example:

```
<concept id="concept_engines">
...
<img id="img_ej25_engine" href="../images/ej25.png"
 width="480px" height="360px" />
...
</concept>

<task>
...
<img conref="#concept_engines/img_ej25_engine"
href="-dita-use-conref-target" />
...
</task>
```

Because the `href` attribute of the `image` element is mandatory, you must set the value of the `href` attribute of the referencing `image` to -dita-use-conref-target.

The conref method has the advantage that attributes are also re-used, reducing some duplication of effort. However, if you deliberately want to have different attributes for different uses of the image, the simple file re-use method can be used.

If you are using figure (`fig`) structures instead of simple images, you can either conref the `image` element or the `fig` element. The method to choose will depend on whether you want to re-use the attributes and elements of the figure element.

In DITA 1.2, you can use the `keyref` feature to indirectly reference an image or figure, as an alternative to conref.

Different graphics for different published media

In many cases, the graphic used for a particular publishing output needs to be different to that used for an alternative output. For example, a high resolution PNG image might be required for the PDF output of a topic, but a smaller JPG image required for an eBook output.

The `keyref` attribute introduced in DITA 1.2 allows different image files to be used for the same illustration when a different map is used. Provided a different map file is used for PDF and eBook outputs in the preceding example, the keyref would point to different image files in each map.

This technique would not be relevant if the same map was being used to generate both outputs.

Using the `conkeyref` attribute would be another strategy, where the figure or image element is transcluded using *conref*, where the conref source file is specified in the ditamap rather than in the `conref` attribute in the topic. Different variants of the ditamap, sharing (through nesting) everything except the `conkeyref` targets, would also be required to complete the process.

> **Note:** Some publishing tools and processes also allow you to swap the images (during processing) with images of the appropriate size and resolution for the target output.

Image alignment, placement, and sizing

The placement of the image on the output page or screen is defined in the `placement` and `align` attributes. The `placement` attribute can be set to inline (placing the image inline with the text in the paragraph in which it is placed) or break (placing the image in its own block, with space above and below it). The `align` attribute has valid values of left, right, center and current. These values specify how the image will be aligned on the page or screen. The `align` attribute only has an effect if the placement is set to break.

To display the image in its own block, use the image element independently of a paragraph element, set the `placement` attribute to break, and the alignment to left, right, or center.

To display an image within a paragraph or other block element, set the `placement` attribute to inline, and either omit the `align` attribute or set it to current (to inherit the alignment settings of the element in which the image is contained).

The `image` element includes `height` and `width` attributes. These attributes are used to store the intended display height and width of the image in the output, expressed in one of a variety of units, including pixels (px), centimetres (cm), points (pt) and inches (in).

Images in titles

Although other `title` elements (including section titles) can technically contain images and figures (in that images within topic and section titles are valid DITA), these structures should be avoided. Titles are used for purposes other than simply rendering headings in the output, and in some uses (such as for running headers in page layout outputs) images in titles will produce undesirable or unintended results.

Callouts

Diagrams are often explained with the aid of *callouts*, which are labels and leader lines or arrows that point out key parts of the illustration. Callouts can be text, or *keyed legends*.

In text callouts, the labels are superimposed on the image. In *keyed* callouts, language independent key numbers or letters are superimposed on the image, with a legend providing the explanations for the callout keys displayed outside the image.

The following figures show the two main approaches to image callouts, text and *keyed*:

Figure 37: Example of text callouts on an illustration

Figure 38: Example of keyed callouts on an illustration

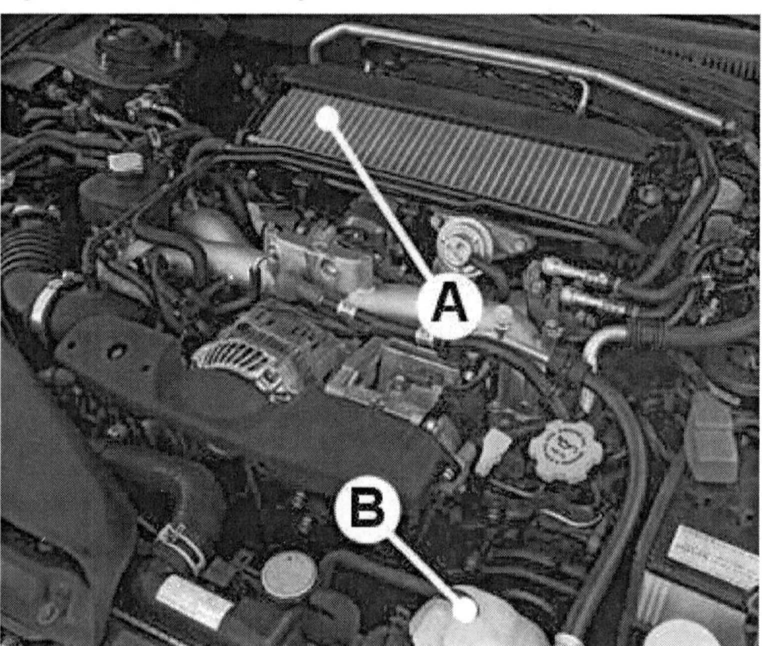

A	intercooler
B	expansion tank

You should prefer the *keyed* method, with the legend stored in a definition list (`dl`) or a `simpletable` structure, within the figure (`fig`) element. Legends are more easily maintained and more easily localized, as the text explanations are stored as text rather than embedded within the image file.

> **Note:** The `fig` element can contain an image, an ordered list, a paragraph and a table. This provides the tools for building a set of labels, a legend, or multiple captions.

An example of a definition list within a figure structure is:

```
<fig>
  <title>Example of keyed callouts on an
illustration</title>
  <image href="../images/callout_key_ej25_turbo.jpg"
width="393px" height="322px">
    <alt>Example of keyed callouts on an
illustration</alt>
```

```
  </image>
        <dl>
          <dlentry>
               <dt>A</dt>
               <dd>intercooler</dd>
          </dlentry>
          <dlentry>
               <dt>B</dt>
               <dd>expansion tank</dd>
          </dlentry>
        </dl>
</fig>
```

Callout keys should use alphabetical characters rather than numerical characters, unless the sequence is important.

Localizing graphics

In many cases, documents written in a DITA environment will be translated to another language. Localization software programs and XML languages work incredibly well together, so the localization process is generally very efficient. However, localization runs into a stumbling block where graphics include words.

The problem is essentially eliminated if the graphic is in *Scalable Vector Graphics* format, because, being an XML format, translatable text can be extracted out of an image and the translated text reinserted.

For raster graphics, where the text in a graphic is made up of uneditable pixels, you should use a key for callouts. The callout therefore becomes a key reference (for example, "A") to the description, which is typically recorded in a table or definition list under the graphic.

Multimedia in DITA topics

Multimedia objects such as Flash animations, Java applets, and video files can be included in DITA content using the `object` element. Obviously, when a topic which includes multimedia is output to paper, the object cannot be properly rendered. You may want to use conditional processing so that multimedia objects are only output to online delivery formats.

The DITA `object` element is based on the HTML `object` element, but with a smaller set of valid attributes. If your DITA authoring tool does not provide good support for embedding objects, you can alternatively use a Web authoring tool to place the `object` in an HTML page, and then copy the HTML `object` code into your DITA topic.

An example of the DITA code to place a Flash animation in a topic is:

```
<object id="anim_ej25" data="../images/ace.swf"
      type="application/x-shockwave-flash"
width="350" height="100">
        <param name="movie" value="../images/
ej25.swf"/>
        <param name="quality" value="high"/>
     </object>
```

Attributes for the DITA `object` element that are common to the HTML `object` element are:

- archive
- classid
- codebase
- codetype
- data
- declare
- dir
- height
- name
- standby
- tabindex
- type
- usemap
- width
- xml:lang

Figures containing tables

Figures will normally contain images or other forms of graphical illustration. However, they can also contain text-based objects such as simple tables (`simpletable` elements), definition lists (`dl` elements), code blocks (`codeblock` elements), message blocks (`msgblock` elements), and long quotations (`lq` elements).

As a simple table can itself contain images, it is also possible to use the `simpletable` structure to create figures comprising multiple images and text fragments, such as a collection of images along with supporting explanatory text.

Example of Code for Table Containing Images in a Figure Structure

```
<fig>
 <title>Screen captures showing
different rendering views</title>
 <simpletable>
  <strow>
   <stentry>
    <image href="../images/
qa_dhtml_before.png">
     <alt>Screen capture showing the
standard display of a topic </alt>
    </image>
   </stentry>
  </strow>
  <strow>
   <stentry>
    <image href="../images/
qa_dhtml_after.png">
     <alt>Screen capture showing the
display of a topic in QA mode</alt>
    </image>
   </stentry>
  </strow>
 </simpletable>
</fig>
```

Image maps

Image maps, also known as *hotspot graphics* and *segmented hypergraphics*, can be defined in DITA content using the `imagemap` element and its child elements. An imagemap element is applied to a standard `image` element. Obviously, when a topic which includes an image map is output to paper, the linking function will be lost; however, the static image will be rendered. You may want to use conditional processing so that image map graphics are only output to online delivery formats.

The DITA `imagemap` element is modeled on the HTML 4.1 `map` element, but uses elements where HTML uses attributes.

Table 2: Comparison of HTML and DITA image map element names

DITA mark-up	HTML mark-up
imagemap element	map element
image element (inside imagemap)	img element (outside map)
area element	area element
shape element	shape attribute of area element
coords element	coords attribute of area element
href attribute of xref element	href attribute of area element
text content of xref element	alt attribute of area element

The imagemap element has two child elements: an image element and an area element. The image element defines the image to which the clickable hotspot areas will be overlaid. The area element contains shape, coords, and xref elements which specify the hotspot co-ordinates and link targets.

An example of the DITA code to place an image map in a topic is:

```
<imagemap>
  <image href="../images/ej25.png" />
  <area>
    <shape>rect</shape>
    <coords>0,10,60,75</coords>
    <xref href="c_intercooler.dita">Intercooler</
xref>
  </area>
  <area>
    <shape>circle</shape>
    <coords>30,120,30</coords>
    <xref href="c_expansion.dita">Expansion tank</
xref>
  </area>
</imagemap>
```

> **Note:** If your DITA authoring tool does not provide good support for creating image maps, you can alternatively use a Web authoring tool to define the map in an HTML page, change the HTML attributes to DITA elements, and then copy the resultant code into your DITA topic.

Image maps are not permitted within a figure (`fig`) structure.

WAI compliance

Graphics in HTML and other online formats must have alternative text representations in order to comply with *Web Accessibility Initiative (WAI)* guidelines (and national laws, such as *US Section 508*).

You must include alternative text representation values in the `alt` attribute of all `image` elements.

If the images are purely presentational in nature, they should be applied via CSS (in the *presentation layer*). When an image is specified within a CSS, there is no capacity to specify alternative text; such images are considered to be simply decorative. This does not breach the WAI recommendations.

When graphics are used to denote notes, warnings, etc, it could be argued that the images contain meaning. Therefore, CSS should not be used to place such images; the HTML `img` element, with a descriptive `alt` attribute, should be used. These labels will be applied by the DITA publishing process; as a DITA author, you only need to apply the correct semantic mark-up, such as the `note` element and its `type` attribute.

Chapter 6: Cross-referencing

What's in this chapter?

- Types of cross-references
- The xref element
- Avoiding in-text cross-references to topics
- Cross-referencing topics and external resources
- Cross-referencing elements in a topic
- Links in related-links sections
- Managing cross-references
- Cross-references in titles

> There is no greater skill a web professional needs to develop than the ability to create quality links. Many websites do not need more publishing. Rather, they need more linking of content in appropriate task journeys. Linking is a complex skill because it requires you to see the task through your customer's eyes.
>
> **Gerry McGovern**

Types of cross-references

In DITA, cross-referencing is more than simple hyperlinking, or references to page numbers or section titles. Topics, paragraphs, sections, steps, figures, tables and many other DITA elements can be cross-referenced, along with resources external to the DITA content such as Web addresses, network files, and e-mail addresses.

Cross-references are implemented primarily through the `xref` element and its `href` attribute. Also key to cross-referencing in DITA is the `id` attribute: only elements with an `id` attribute can be cross-referenced.

Cross-referencing features can sometimes be found in unexpected places. For example, the `lq` element includes an `href` attribute, used for storing the URL of the source of the quotation, if applicable. The `source` element in a topic's prolog and the `link` element in the `related-`

`links` section also have an `href` attribute to store the URL of the original source of the topic content, if applicable.

Cross-references to different elements are resolved, when the collection is processed (published), in different ways. For example, a cross-reference to a `step` element may be rendered as the step number in the output.

The DITA syntax for referencing elements within the same topic is `#[topicid]/[elementid]`.

Avoid generic cross-references to simple paragraphs; instead, cross-references should be to the topic as a whole.

The `xref` element

The cross-reference (`xref`) element allows you to link text within the body of a DITA topic to different *target* resources. Although you can manually specify the text for the cross-reference or link itself, in most cases you should let DITA *calculate* the text based on the type of resource you are linking to. You specify that you want DITA to calculate the cross-reference text by leaving the element empty. For example, if you cross-reference a figure (*fig*) element, the cross-reference text may be automatically generated as `Figure 15`. If you provide text within the `xref` element, that text will be used as the cross-reference text.

Likewise, if you cross-reference a topic, and leave the `xref` element empty, the target topic title will be used as the cross-reference text. For examples of automatically-generated cross-reference text, see Sample topic - cross-references.

The cross-reference (`xref`) element has the following attributes:

href
: nominates the address of the resource to be referenced, such as a topic, a block within a topic, a PDF file, an external Web resource, or an e-mail address.

type
: describes the type of resource being referenced, such as `concept` for a DITA concept topic, `li` for a list item in a list within a topic, `fn` for a footnote within a topic, `fig` for a figure within a topic, or `table` for a table within a topic.

format describes the file format of resource being referenced, such as `dita` for a DITA topic, `pdf` for a PDF file, and `html` for a Web resource.

scope indicates whether the referenced resource is within the same document as the topic (local), or whether it is external to the document (external).

The syntax of the `href` attribute is illustrated through the following examples:

- Reference to a topic (or the first topic in a composite (*ditabase*) topic): `"file.dita"`
- Reference to a specific topic in a composite (*ditabase*) topic: `"file.dita#topicid"`
- Reference to an element inside a DITA topic: `"file.dita#topicid/elementid"`
- Reference to an element in a ditamap: `"collection.ditamap#map-branch"`
- Reference to an image: `"example.png"`
- Reference to an external resource: `"http://www.example.org"`

Avoiding in-text cross-references to topics

The ditamap's purpose is not limited to specifying the contents of a collection. Automatic inter-topic links are also generated from the ditamap topic hierarchy, and a relationship table section in the ditamap can further extend this automatic linking.

When the same topic appears in a different ditamap, its links will be determined by the hierarchy and relationship table in that different ditamap. In other words, topic-linking is not distributed across many topics, but centralized in the ditamap. This makes maintenance far more efficient.

Cross-references to other topics within paragraphs of a topic can be problematic if the cross-referenced target is not always distributed with the source topic. This can lead to broken links or false assumptions about links being in place.

You should therefore define inter-topic cross-references in the ditamap, using the relationship table (`reltable`) feature.

There is some evidence that linking outside the paragraph text in this way may be more effective.

> I've found that the most effective links are written like headings, not part of sentences at all. I've found that putting links in sentences reduces readability and clickability.
>
> **Gerry McGovern**

Usability tests on the effectiveness of links conducted by Jared Spool support the view that externalized links are more effective than inline, embedded links. Spool's study concluded that:

- Links are less usable when embedded in the text.
- Longer links are more effective than shorter ones.
- People scan for target words - the scent of information.

Cross-referencing topics and external resources

Format of `href` attribute in cross-references

The resources being referenced in `xref`, `link`, `lq`, `glossref`, and `source` elements are specified in the `href` attribute.

A *URI*, or *Uniform Resource Indicator*, is a standard for referencing resources on the Internet. The similar term *URL*, or *Uniform Resource Locator*, means a specific type of *URI* where the location and the means of retrieving the resource are both incorporated in the address. For example, the *URL* `http://store.scriptorium.com/items/Books/list.htm` nominates the address of the resource and the protocol to use to retrieve it (in this case, *http*). In general, however, most people use the terms interchangeably!

Files on a file server or network drive on a local network can be referenced using the URI convention. Most DITA authoring tools will let you browse for the resource you want to reference, and then format the address in the correct UNC format. For example, the address of a file on a network server must be prefixed with the protocol `smb://`.

You must use (forward) slash characters for path separators. Do not use backslashes. Such file references are URIs in DITA, not file paths. The backslash is an illegal character in URIs. When referencing resources on a network server, prefix the UNC path with `smb://`.

You cannot use an ampersand (&) character in an `href` attribute. If the URL being referenced contains an ampersand character, the `&` character escape should be used to indicate that character.

Links to non-DITA resources

The four most important attributes in the cross-reference (`xref`) element are `href`, `type`, `scope` and `format`.

When linking to non-DITA resources such as PDF files or Web addresses, the `scope` attribute describes whether the linked resource is treated as part of the DITA collection or external to it. This setting will ultimately determine how the HTML output code will be formed during the publishing process, and then how the browser will handle the link. The `format` attribute describes the type of resource being linked to.

The main `scope` attribute values are:

local the resource forms part of the content collection (and will typically be opened in the current browser when it is output to a hypertext form)

external the resource is managed separately to the content collection (and will typically be opened in a new browser or tab when it is output to a hypertext form)

> **Note:** The other valid `scope` attribute of peer is similar to local, but is used when the linked resource is not available at build time. It is only relevant when linking to DITA resources.

The valid `format` attribute values for non-DITA resources are:

html the non-DITA file format of the linked resource is HTML or XHTML

pdf the non-DITA file format of the linked resource is PDF

txt the non-DITA file format of the linked resource is plain text

file type the three letter file extension of the non-DITA file format of the linked resource (for example, `ppt` and `odt`)

An example of the code for a local and an external cross-reference link is:

```
<xref href="somefile.html" format="html"
scope="local" />
<xref href="somefile.doc" format="doc"
scope="external" />
<xref href="http://abc.com/intro.htm" format="html"
scope="external" />
```

Linking in a new window

If a topic being referenced in an *xref* is external to the document content, the `xref` element's `scope` attribute should be set to `external` to semantically identify this relationship.

If you want a cross-referenced Web or external resource to open in a new window, code the `xref` as in the example:

```
<xref href="..../somefile.html" format="html"
scope="external" />
```

> **Note:** Opening external target resources in a new window is a processing function, and is therefore dependent upon the publishing tool used and its configuration. This behavior is not part of the DITA standard itself.

Links to glossary terms

In DITA content, the `term` element is used to semantically identify technical or specialist terms, acronyms, abbreviations, and other items of jargon that need to be defined to be understood by some readers. The terms used in a document are normally defined in a separate glossary section.

The glossary entry (`glossentry`) information type can be used to define individual terms; those topics can then be collected into a glossary section in the ditamap.

Terms used within normal topic text can be linked, as part of the publishing process, to any corresponding definition of that term in a `glossentry` topic. Linking is accomplished using the `keyref` attribute within the `term` element, and then defining the topic associated with the `keyref` in the ditamap, through `glosskey` elements. (The `keyref` attribute was introduced in DITA 1.2.)

For example, the mark-up `<term keyref="eoy">EOY</term>` establishes the association between the term "EOY" and the glossary topic with a `keys` attribute of `eoy`. The related map entry may be `<glossref keys="eoy" href="eoy_nz.dita"/>`.

Indirect linking with keys

Indirection is an indirect method of linking, introduced in DITA 1.2. Instead of referring to the address of the resource, you refer to a key, which in turn refers to the address of the resource. As the key can be stored away from the topic in the ditamap, the same link or reference in a topic can point to different targets, depending upon the ditamap in which the topic is used.

Indirection opens up the opportunity to:

- redirect a link to a new target if an override is defined in the ditamap
- redirect a `conref` to a new target
- add text to a term or keyword
- turn terms into links

Key values are defined in a ditamap using the syntax `key="`*`target URI`*`"`. To refer to a key in a topic, usually inside a cross-reference (`xref`), `term` or `image` element, a `keyref` attribute is used instead of the direct `href` attribute. Indirection can also be used for content reference *transclusion* by using the `conkeyref` attribute in place of the direct `conref` attribute.

If the key referred to in a `keyref` attribute is not defined in the ditamap, the target reverts to the value of the `href` attribute, if defined.

For example, if the `alpha key` in the following cross-reference is not defined in the ditamap, the link will be created to `abc.dita`.

```
<xref keyref="alpha" href="abc.dita">Alpha</xref>
```

If the `alpha key` does exist, the `href` attribute will be ignored. (The `keyref` overrides the `href`.)

Figure 39: Indirection schematic

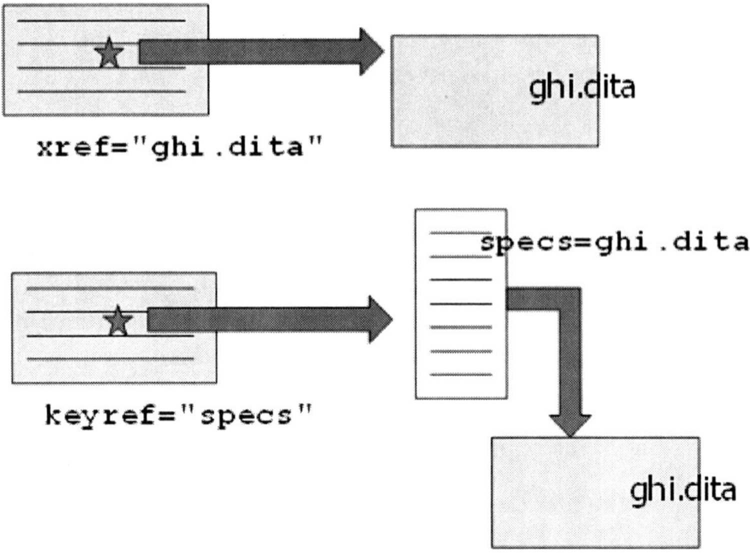

Indirection has the effect of moving context from the topic to the map, which allows the topic to be re-used in more places.

Cross-referencing elements in a topic

Cross-referencing figures

When referring a reader to a figure (an image or illustration), you should not hard-code the figure number. In most editing environments, you won't know what the sequential figure number will be until the ditamap is processed to a deliverable document.

You must always use the `xref` element to cross-reference figures, with the `type` attribute set to `fig`.

Cross-references to figures will typically be rendered as the local language word for "Figure", followed by the figure's sequential number in the topic (for hypertext outputs) or in the publication (for page layout documents). Because the figure number is not hard-coded, it will be recalculated each time the ditamap containing the topic is processed.

An example of the syntax of a cross-reference to a figure with an id attribute of "fig_ej25_engine" in the same topic is:

```
<xref href="#concept_ej25/fig_sample_darwin"
type="fig"/>
```

You cannot cross-reference images, so if cross-references are important for your document, use figures rather than simple images. You should include a title element in all figure elements, as the title is used in the generation of cross-reference text in some publishing processes.

Cross-referencing tables

When referring a reader to a table, you should not hard-code the table number. In most editing environments, you won't know what the sequential table number will be until the ditamap is processed to a deliverable document.

You must always use the xref element to cross-reference tables, with the type attribute set to table.

Cross-references to tables will typically be rendered as the local language word for "Table", followed by the table's sequential number in the topic (for hypertext outputs) or in the publication (for page layout documents). Because the table number is not hard-coded, it will be recalculated each time the ditamap containing the topic is processed.

An example of the syntax of a cross-reference to a table with an id attribute of "table_perf_data" in the same topic is:

```
<xref href="#concept_ej25_perf/perfdata"
type="table"/>
```

You cannot cross-reference simple tables, partly because they do not have titles (necessary for labeling the table with a table number.) If cross-references are important for your document, use tables rather than simple tables. You should include a title element in all table elements, as the title is used in the generation of cross-reference text in some publishing processes.

Cross-referencing to a page number

When you cross-reference to a topic, or to an element within a topic, and then publish to a page layout format such as PDF, the publishing processor will typically calculate the page number of the referenced topic or element.

For example, a cross-reference to a figure will typically be rendered, when published to PDF, as: `Figure 1: ` *`Title of Figure`* `(see page ` *`number`*`).`

DITA is designed around the concept of the separation of content and form. Page numbers are part of the form, and are therefore always generated as part of the publishing process that converts the DITA source to a reading format output.

Avoid cross-referencing simple paragraphs or other points in a topic in order to generate a page number reference. Cross-references should be to the topic as a whole.

Cross-referencing a step

When referring a reader to a step in a task, you should not hard-code the step number. In different contexts (such as when the content is filtered or transcluded) the step number may be different, or if a step is added, there is a high risk that the hard-coded reference won't be updated.

You must always use the `xref` element to cross-reference steps, with the `type` attribute set to `li`. (The `li` element is the ancestor of the `step` element.)

You can only reference a step by its `id` attribute; therefore, before you can cross-reference to a step, you must ensure that the `step` element's `id` attribute has a value.

The following example illustrates how to cross-reference a step number. Don't include any text in the `xref` element, otherwise this text will be rendered (in most publishing tools), not the step number.

```
<task id="keypad1">
...
<step id="a">
      <cmd>..</cmd>
      </step>
      <step>
      <cmd>Repeat step <xref href="#keypad1/a"
type="li" /> until the red light displays.</cmd>
      </step>
...
</task>
```

Referring to a step in another topic is almost identical; the difference is that the href attribute will include the file name of the other topic. Again, you must set the type attribute to li.

```
<cmd>Complete step <xref href="c_panel.dita#keypad2/
b" type="li" /> of
the PIN recovery procedure.</cmd>
```

Cross-referencing a transcluded element

If you need to cross-reference a transcluded element (that is, the target of a conref), you should cross-reference the instance of the conref, and not the original element.

For example, in the following content:

```
<concept id="fuel_filter">
...
<p>For more information, see <xref type="fig".../>.</
p>
...
<fig id="fig_fuel_sys"
conref="conref_source.dita#conref_figs/fuelsys"
</fig>
...
</concept>
```

there are two fig elements. The first fig element, fig_fuel_sys, is the element containing the conref, or the referencing element. The other fig element, fuelsys in the topic named conref_source.dita, is the source of the conref, or the referenced element. The cross-reference in this scenario must be to the referencing element, and not the referenced conref source. This means the cross-reference code must be:

```
<xref href="#fuel_filter/fig_fuel_sys" type="fig" />
```

Links in related-links sections

There are three methods through which links can be included in DITA content:

- inserting xref elements at any point within the body of a topic
- inserting links in a related-links section within a topic, outside the body of the topic
- defining link relationships between topics through relationship tables in the ditamap

The most effective method for most documents is the relationship table approach. However, if the cross-references will always be appropriate for the topic, regardless of the context in which it is used, then the `related-links` section can be used.

The `related-links` section is technically metadata, and is structured within the topic but outside the body section. It is made up of `link` elements, which are similar in function to an `xref` element.

Structure of the `related-links` section

One of the methods of defining links in DITA content is through a `related-links` section at the end of a topic, outside the topic body.

The `related-links` section has the following structure:

```
<topic>
  <title>...</title>
  <body>
  ...
  </body>
  <related-links>
    <link href="URL of referenced topic or resource">
      <linktext>Display text for link</linktext>
    </link>
    <link>...</link>
    .
    .
    .
  </related-links>
</topic>
```

To better organize links, the link elements can be grouped into `linklist` and `linkpool` container elements. These container elements allow metadata attributes to be applied to a set of links as a whole.

For example, if you wanted to nominate that all links in a `linklist` have a `product` attribute of `lite`, you could use the following mark-up:

```
<related-links>
  <linklist product="lite">
    <link>...</link>
    <link>...</link>
    .
    .
  </linklist>
```

The linklist container is used when the order of the links is important, as that order will be maintained when the content is processed to an output format. The linkpool container does not imply any particular order. (In this respect, linklist is like an ordered list, while linkpool is like an unordered list.)

When in a linklist container, links in the output will typically be displayed without a heading, and in the same order as the links are defined in the linklist. When in a linkpool container, or when not contained (as simple link elements within the related-links section), links in the output will be grouped according to their information type (such as under headings of "Related Concepts", "Related Tasks", "Related References", and "Related Information").

Within the link structure, the linktext element, which defines the display text for the link, is optional. When there is no linktext element, the title of the referenced DITA topic will be used as the display text for the link.

You should not include the linktext element when linking to DITA topics. This will force the title of the target to be used as the link text, and ensures that the link text matches the target topic title. However, for links to non-DITA resources such as Web sites or PDF documents, you should define the link text.

Note:

Some sample links are included in the related-links section of this topic. These links will only appear in hypertext versions of *The DITA Style Guide*. The code for the sample links is:

Type of link	Code
Link to another DITA topic with no linktext element	<link href="c_Scope_Attribute. dita"> </link>
Link to another DITA topic with a linktext element	<link href="c_Scope_Attribute. dita> <linktext>Alternative link to Scope Attribute

Type of link	Code
	</linktext> </link>
Link to an external Web site	<link format="html" scope="external" href="http://www.hyperwrite.com/"> <linktext>HyperWrite Web Site</linktext> </link>

The three sample links are included in the related-links section twice: the first set of links is not contained in a container element, while the second set of links is contained within a linklist element.

The desc element in links

The desc element inside the link element holds a description of the link target. The desc content is not rendered as content, but will typically appear as tooltip text in online outputs.

The importance attribute and related links

When writing a task topic, you will often include a pre-requisities (prereq) element. In some cases, pre-requisites for the task will include other procedures, described in separate topics. Logically, these pre-requisite task topics should be linked to in the prereq block.

Rather than including a link to an associated topic in an xref element in the prereq block, you should create a link element in the related-links section, and then set the importance attribute of the link element to required. In typical output processing, this will result in the link being rendered at the end of the prereq block.

The linkinfo element

The linkinfo element can be used within the ordered link list (linklist) element to provide an explanation of the purpose of the list of links. The linkinfo block typically appears after the list of links in the output reading format.

When used in conjunction with a `title` element also within the `linklist`, you can create a brief description of a process in the `related-links` section. However, you should always prefer creating small task topics, or stub topics with generated links to *child* tasks.

Managing cross-references

Cross-referencing a ditamap

Creating a cross-reference to a ditamap may at first seem to be unremarkable. On reflection, however, cross-referencing a ditamap is problematic.

A ditamap is a specification for a published document, or for part of a document (if nested or modular ditamaps are being used). As such, the ditamap itself contains no content, and it doesn't make sense to link to nothing! More logically, the cross-reference should be to the first topic referenced by the ditamap.

The solution is not as clear-cut as that, unfortunately. There are times when you might want to cross-reference a chapter, as in "described in Chapter 2". Chapter infrastructures are defined in the map, and although they are not content, they are still likely targets of a cross-reference. In any case, DITA topics are intended to be context-agnostic, so cross-referencing a ditamap would restrict that topic's use to publications where the referenced ditamap is also included.

Further, DITA has no clear mechanism for cross-referencing ditamap `topicref` elements.

Avoid cross-references to ditamaps. If required, it may be better to cross-reference to the published version of the ditamap, such as the PDF location or Web URL.

Removing related links from the output

When DITA content is processed to HTML output, links to related topics (if any) are typically placed (by the publishing process) at the bottom of each topic. Some publishing tools generate these links with a *Cascading Style Sheet (CSS)* class of `ullinks` for the `ul` or `ol` element, and a class of `ulchildlink` for each of the `li` elements.

If you don't want these links to appear in the output, there are a few options.

Firstly, it's important to understand why the links are there. The links are either generated because the topic has a `related-links` element, or because related links have been automatically generated based on the ditamap topic hierarchies (parent/child relationships) or relationship table links.

If you don't want the links generated from the `related-links` section, you may consider removing the section from the topic, or using conditional processing to exclude it.

If you don't want the links generated from the hierarchy, set the `linking` attribute of the `map` or top-level `topicref` elements in the ditamap to none.

If you don't want the links generated from the relationship table in your ditamap, set the `linking` attribute of the `reltable` element to none.

An alternative method is to nominate a custom stylesheet for the output, and set that stylesheet so that classes of `ullinks` and `ulchildlink` have a CSS styling of `display=none`.

Conditions in cross-references

If you need to cross-reference different resources for different publication variants, use the `audience` attribute to define these conditions. For example, if the PDF version of the output links to a different resource than the Help version, you could include two adjacent `xref` elements, one with the `audience` attribute set to `pdf_user`, and the other set to `help_user`.

For DITA 1.2 and above, the `keyref` mechanism should be used in preference to duplicating and conditionalizing elements.

If you are using cross-references in conjunction with conditional processing, positioning an in-text cross-reference (`xref`) element at the end of a sentence makes it easier to exclude.

For example, if a cross-reference is to be included in the Web rendition of a DITA collection, but excluded from the PDF rendition, then `audience` attribute might be used to differentiate the PDF-only text.

The code:

```
<p>The coolant expansion tank is attached to
the firewall<ph audience="help_user">, as shown in
<xref href="c_engine_bay#eng_bay/fig_coolant_system"
type="fig">.</ph>
</p>
```

might be rendered in the output as `The coolant expansion tank is attached to the firewall.` when the `help_user` content is excluded, and as `The coolant expansion tank is attached to the firewall, as shown in Figure 3.` otherwise.

Cross-references in titles

The `title` element cannot directly contain an `xref` element, primarily because titles are used in many different presentational contexts, some of which do not support child elements. For example, the `title` element of a DITA topic may become the `title` element in the `head` section of an output XHTML file, which must be plain text. Likewise, the title element of a DITA topic may be used as the basis for link text in its parent topic.

Including child elements in titles therefore reduces the opportunities for re-use, increases the risk of a transformation error caused by mis-interpretation of the mark-up, and complicates what should be a simple semantic element.

However, it **is** technically possible to embed `xref` or other child elements within a `title` element by nesting them within an (allowed) `ph` element. While the `title` element cannot contain `xref` elements, it **can** contain `ph` elements, and `ph` elements can contain `xref` elements.

> **Tip:** Carefully weigh up the implications before using this workaround.

Chapter 7: Content re-use

What's in this chapter?

- Content re-use definition
- Re-use and the DITA Maturity Model
- The content reference (conref) attribute
- Re-use practices
- Variables
- Organizing re-use topics and elements
- Embedded topics and ditamaps
- Advanced conref principles

> Reuse, reuse, reuse, reuse... content reuse is key to content management so it bears repeating repeating repeating. Content reuse means that you can write content once and use it wherever required, but it also means that you have to write content consistently so that it can be reused.
>
> **Pamela Kostur, The Rockley Group**

Content re-use definition

The term *content re-use* means different things to different authors and tool vendors, just as the term *single-sourcing* means different things. Sometimes, those terms are used as glib marketing jargon. DITA supports a maximal implementation of content re-use.

Content re-use is achieved through the following strategies:

- Creating multiple deliverable documents from the same source project.
- Assembling a deliverable document by defining the sequence and hierarchy of content from topics selected from a shared repository.
- Defining conditional publishing rules, where content can be omitted or included depending on the specification of the deliverable document.
- Automated processing of a document's source to extract and re-assemble the content when creating a deliverable document.

- Transcluding content snippets from one topic into another topic.
- Using separately-maintained variables for repeated words or phrases.

Re-use and the DITA Maturity Model

The *DITA Maturity Model*[2] proposed by Michael Priestley and Amber Swope suggests that there are six levels of DITA adoption that an organization can embrace.

The six levels are:

- topics
- scalable re-use
- specialization and customization
- automation and integration
- semantics on demand
- unified semantic ecosystem

The second level, beyond simply using DITA as a topic format, is characterizedcharacterised by the introduction of re-use. In other words, re-use should be one of the first DITA features that you adopt. A good understanding of re-use, and in particular how the *conref* (or content reference) idea works, is required for DITA best practice.

The content reference (`conref`) attribute

In DITA, content can be re-used at the topic level (by using one topic in many ditamaps), at the block level, or at the phrase level. Any DITA element, be it a paragraph, a table, a task pre-requisite, a user interface control, a term, a cross-reference, or any other tagged chunks, can be re-used elsewhere. The mechanism for block and phrase level re-use is the *content reference*, or *conref*.

The key to content referencing, or *transclusion*, is the ability to identify a chunk of content using a simple naming structure.

A content reference is specified by entering the address of the content to be re-used in the `conref` attribute of the element into which it will be

[2] Just Systems Whitepaper, http://na.justsystems.com/files/Whitepaper-DITA_MM.pdf

included or *transcluded*. The `conref` attribute value has the following syntax:

```
topicfilename#topicid/elementid
```

where *topicfilename* is the file name of the topic containing the content to be transcluded, *topicid* is the `id` attribute of the topic, and *elementid* is the `id` attribute of the element to be re-used. (This naming convention is also used for cross-referencing and other types of linking.)

For example, if the source of the content to be transclude is a paragraph (p) element with an `id` attribute of `intercooler_temperature`, in a topic with a file name of `c_intercooler.dita` and an `id` attribute of `concept_turbo_intercooler`, then the referencing paragraph element will be coded as:

```
<p
conref="c_intercooler.dita#concept_turbo_intercooler/
intercooler_temperature"/>
```

The conref idea originated in SGML.

Re-use practices

To best take advantage of content re-use, you should adopt practices to reduce the impediments, increase the opportunities for re-use, and to make the process of re-using easier.

Writing for re-use

In a linear writing environment, you tend to write in the context of the document you are creating. In modular writing, the writing needs to be removed from the context of its use. A modular topic might be used in different manuals, and in entirely different contexts. A description of a memory card may end up in a camera manual, a Netbook Help system, and a mobile phone Web-based user guide.

In DITA, any *taggable* element can be re-used through the *conref* mechanism. This means that paragraphs (block elements) or phrases (inline elements) can be re-used. For example, a `note` block might be used in multiple topics, and even more than once in an individual topic. Likewise, a procedural step, or a product name, might be a re-usable element.

In a DITA authoring environment, you must therefore assume that almost everything you write may end up being re-used elsewhere. You must avoid including context in your writing, as context restricts the ability to re-use.

For example, you should avoid phrasing such as "in the following paragraphs", or "as discussed earlier", or "in the diagram below".

You should also avoid using *restrictive references* where possible. For example, a step command such as "Click Print in the navigation pane on the left" restricts the re-use of that step to cases where the Print button is located in the navigation pane on the left. While "Click Print" or "Click Print in the navigation panel" might sacrifice a little clarity, the benefits of re-use (including editing and translation efficiency) are usually worth the trade.

It could be argued that making compromises to writing style in order to improve the opportunities for re-use results in poorer writing. However, the writing of technical documents is inextricably linked with the business requirements of budgets and deadlines. Trade-offs are common in technical documentation, so the trade-off between writing style and re-use is just another.

Re-use guidelines

When writing in a DITA environment, at topic level rather than document level, there are a few guidelines you can follow to make re-use easier by adopting the following guidelines.

- Avoid the use of "previous", "next", "earlier", and "later" (such as in "More information on the product limitations are discussed later"). Those referenced topics may not be included in all collections, or may be included in a different sequence.
- Don't use sequential numbers in file names; rather, use descriptive names. (Use `ej20_engine_schematic.png` rather than `fig1.png`.)
- Avoid including branding in graphics.

- Avoid including context within explanatory paragraphs or steps. For example, don't write "The EJ20 engine of the Supara Impress is naturally aspirated"; rather write "The EJ20 engine is naturally aspirated".
- Move contextual information to its own paragraph (or *context* element, for task topics). In the EJ20 example preceding, the information about what models of car use the EJ20, and other information relevant to the association between EJ20 and Supara, could be written into a separate paragraph. When the content needs to be re-used in a manual for a differently badged product manual, that context paragraph can be filtered out and the remaining non-contextual content re-used.

Valid referencing elements

Conref transclusions involve two elements: the *referencing element* and the *referenced element.* The *referencing element* is the element that will be re-using the content in the *referenced element* (the source of the re-usable content).

When the element being transcluded requires particular attributes or child elements, then these attributes and elements must also be included in the referencing element code.

For example, a `step` element **must** contain at least one `cmd` element. Therefore, the following mark-up would be invalid DITA because the `cmd` element is missing.

```
<step conref="t_starting.dita#t120/sec_code" />
```

Instead, a "dummy" `cmd` element must be included for the mark-up to be valid, as shown in the following.

```
<step conref="t_starting.dita#t120/sec_code"><cmd /
></step>
```

If an attribute is mandatory in a transcluded element, such at the `tmtype` attribute in the trademark (`tm`) element, the referencing element must include the attribute. However, a special attribute value of -dita-use-conref-target can be used to maintain the validity of the element, and specify that the referenced source element's attributes be used in the transclusion.

The mark-up of a referencing element with a mandatory attribute would therefore follow the pattern in the example:

```
<tm conref="conref_source.dita#names12/var_suparu"
 tmtype="-dita-use-conref-target" />
```

If you are using constraints, a feature introduced in DITA 1.2, you must take care to avoid *conreffing* elements from an unconstrained topic to a constrained topic. (In general, referencing an unconstrained source topic element from a constrained topic will only work if the constraint type is marked as weak, not strict.)

The -dita-use-conref-target attribute value

The attributes on some DITA elements are mandatory, such as the trademark type (`tmtype`) attribute of a trademark (`tm`) element. When you conref such an element, the source element's attributes are not ascribed to the referencing element. The referencing conref element is therefore invalid, because it lacks the mandatory attribute.

For example, the trademark element:

```
<tm id="tm_hyperwrite" tmtype="reg">HyperWrite</tm>
```

would logically be referenced using conref as:

```
<tm conref="#about_company/tm_hyperwrite"/>
```

However, because that referencing `tm` element does not a `tmtype` attribute, it is invalid.

To circumvent the invalidity, you could also include the attribute in the referencing element, as:

```
<tm conref="#about_company/tm_hyperwrite"
tmtype="reg"/>
```

However, this involves repeating the same information, which goes against the ideal of re-using rather than copying.

DITA elements that have mandatory attributes, or that have *enumerated* values (that is, a fixed choice of valid values), also have a -dita-use-conref-target value. This value forces the attribute value of the conref source (the referenced element) being used in the referencing element.

A conref to a trademark could therefore be coded as:

```
<tm conref="#about_company/tm_hyperwrite" tmtype="-
dita-use-conref-target"/>
```

Re-using content from different elements

You cannot re-use the text of one element directly inside the text of another.

For example, you cannot conref the text of a paragraph (`p`) element into a `note` element as in:

```
<p id="wiper_blades">...</p>
...

<note conref="conref_source.dita#cref_terms/
wiper_blades" />
```

The referenced element must match the referencing element.

When transcluding phrase elements, you can work around the matching elements requirement that by wrapping the text to be re-used in a generic phrase (`ph`) element. You can then re-use the `ph` element within other elements.

For example, if you want to re-use the words "STi Web Site" within normal paragraph text, as a citation (`cite`) element, and within cross-reference elements, you can use the approach:

```
<ph id="sti_web">STi Web Site</ph>
...

<p>
  The <ph conref="conref_source.dita#cref_terms/
sti_web" />...
</p>

<p>
  As listed on the <cite><ph
conref="conref_source.dita#cref_terms/sti_web" /></
cite>
</p>

<xref href="http://sti.Supara.com.au"
scope="external" format="html">
        <ph conref="conref_source.dita#cref_terms/
sti_web" />
</xref>
```

DITA 1.2 introduced the `text` element. Use this element in preference to the `ph` element for re-using text snippets.

Nested content references

Nested conrefs are content references within other content references. For example, a company name variable might be transcluded into a product name variable.

For example, the company name "Supara" might be transcluded by itself, or within the full product name "Supara Impress XRW", which itself includes the product trademark.

Figure 40: Nested conref principles

Full Product Name phrase (ph)

Company Name phrase (ph)

Product Trademark (tm)

The DITA code for such a nested conref might be:

```
<p>The <ph conref="co.dita#corpnames/var_xrw" /> was
released in 1990.</p>
```

where the `var_xrw` `ph` element in `co.dita` is:

```
<ph id="var_xrw">
  <ph conref="#corpnames/co"/> <tm
conref="#corpnames/impxrw" tm="-dita-use-conref-
target"/>
</ph>
```

and the *co* and *impxrw* elements are:

```
<ph id="co">Supara</ph>
...
<tm id="impxrw" tmtype="reg" tmowner="FJ Heavy
Industries">Impress XRW</tm>
```

DITA 1.2 introduced the `text` element. Use this element in preference to the `ph` element for re-using text snippets.

Variables

Variables are often used phrases (such as product names) that are re-used by replacing the value of the variable at the time the information is published.

Variables using *conref* and filtering

In the context of single-source publishing, a variable is an element that is used throughout the content of a publication in place of a normal fixed unit of text. When the document is published, the variable element is replaced with a nominated phrase or block of text. Variables allow numerous text changes to be made with very little effort.

For example, documentation might be required for a product sold under two brand names, *Legend* and *Liberty*. Instead of *hard-coding* the product name, a variable of *brand_name* might be used whenever the product is mentioned in the text. During the publishing of the documentation for the *Liberty* brand, the *brand_name* variable is replaced with the word "Liberty."

In DITA, variables are implemented through the *conref* and *ditaval* filtering features. The variable is coded as *conreffed* element, such as `<ph conref="abc.dita#product" />`. The *conref* source is coded using metadata attributes that can be used for filtering, such as:

```
<ph id="product>
  <ph product="Liberty">Liberty</ph>
  <ph product="Legend">Legend</ph>
</ph>
```

When the content is published, the conditional filtering in the *ditaval* can be set so that only the applicable product name element is included in the output.

Variables using indirection

The `keyref` feature introduced in DITA 1.2 allows re-used terms or phrases that often vary according to output publication to be managed more easily. You can collect such *variable* terms into a `keydef` section in the ditamap, and then use the `keyword` and its `keyref` attribute to re-use them. You must also nominate a *fallback* value, in case the relevant key is not defined in any ditamap in which the topic is referenced.

Because the content model of the `keyword` element in a ditamap is different to that in a topic, you have to contain the ditamap keyword element within `topicmeta` and `keywords` elements.

As a simple example, a generic car component topic can include the name of the specific car in whose manual the topic appears. A sentence in the generic topic may be:

```
Your <keyword keyref="car_name">car<keyword> has
high intensity discharge headlamps.
```

If that topic is included in a ditamap with a key defined as:

```
<keydef keys="car_name">
  <topicmeta><keywords><keyword>Liberty</keyword></
keywords></topicmeta>
</keydef>
```

the topic will be rendered as:

```
Your Liberty has high intensity discharge headlamps.
```

In this example, if the ditamap didn't have a definition for the `car_name` key, the word "car", which is the value of the `keyword` element in the topic, would be used in the output.

> **Note:** You may find it easier to manage keys in the ditamap if you use a separate, nested ditamap to contain the keys only.

Using internal entities for variables

Internal entities function as typing shortcuts in XML documents. They allow a string or phrase to be defined in the head of the XML file, and then used in the body of the content using a shortcut notation. For example, the phrase "Supara Lumberer" may be defined as `<!ENTITY lumberer "Supara Lumberer">`, and that *lumberer* entity used within the document as `&lumberer;`. They can theoretically be used for creating variables.

Do not use internal entities. Their use inhibits interchange, and they are technically difficult for authors to work with. They are also changed during XSL transformations, resulting in inconsistent output results.

Organizing re-use topics and elements

Re-use of content is easier for the author to accomplish if the elements to be re-used are carefully organized in predictable locations.

Managing re-use files

DITA can re-use an existing document fragment (essentially, any element) from another topic through the *conref* feature. For example, a common warning needs only to be written once, and then can be re-used throughout a document suite. The *conref* source can either be left in the topic in which they happen to be first used, or moved to a dedicated re-usable content topic, whose only purpose is to store re-usable fragments.

In nearly all cases, the best approach is to store re-usable components in a dedicated re-use topic, in a common location. This is known as the *centralized approach*; referenced conref source fragments are stored in a single location.

The centralized strategy of using one or more files to hold elements that you want to re-use reduces dependencies. If you give a set of DITA topics to another writer, you only need to provide the set of topics plus the re-use file. You don't need to hunt around to find other topics that might contain re-used elements. The centralized strategy also simplifies the associations (linkages) between files.

You should assign file names prefixed with `conref_` to topics that are only used as stores for re-use elements.

Figure 41: Example of conref source files within a conref folder

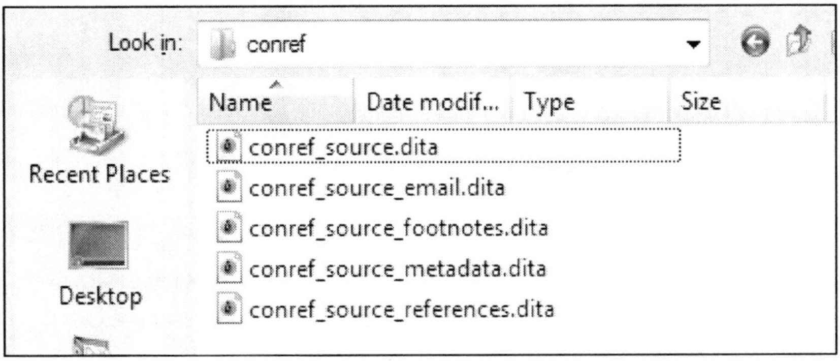

If you are using one conref source topic for all your re-use elements, use the *ditabase* information type for this purpose. This information type can contain both common elements and elements specific to different information types. For larger documentation repositories, you should organize your re-use elements into separate files for separate purposes, such as one file for warnings, one file for variables, one file for steps, and so on.

You should also make a practice of including the dedicated re-use topic(s) in the collection's ditamap, with the `toc` attribute set to no, the `linking` attribute to none, and the `print` attribute set to no. Including the re-use topic in the map provides a reminder that the collection uses that specific re-use topic, and to include the topic when sending the collection source files to another author. This is especially important for large repositories of information, or where your *CMS* uses the ditamap as a basis for copying or checking out files. If you have more than a handful of re-use topics, you should use a nested map to collect those re-use topics together, and then reference that map file in your collection's ditamap.

Ideally, *conref* topics should be stored in their own folder at one directory level lower than the ditamap, or loosely in the same directory as the ditamap.

Organizing elements within re-use topics

Easy-to-identify `id` attributes should be used for re-use elements. In choosing names, you should prefix the `id` values to indicate the purpose of the element, such as:

var_	for short re-use phrases and variables
term_	for terms and definitions
step_	for task steps
warning_	for warning notes
fig_	for figures

To provide a reference for how re-use elements are meant to be used, you may choose to organize re-use phrases (or *variables*) into tables, where a description of the element's intended use can be documented alongside the re-use content.

Figure 42: Conref source file with re-use elements organized with a table

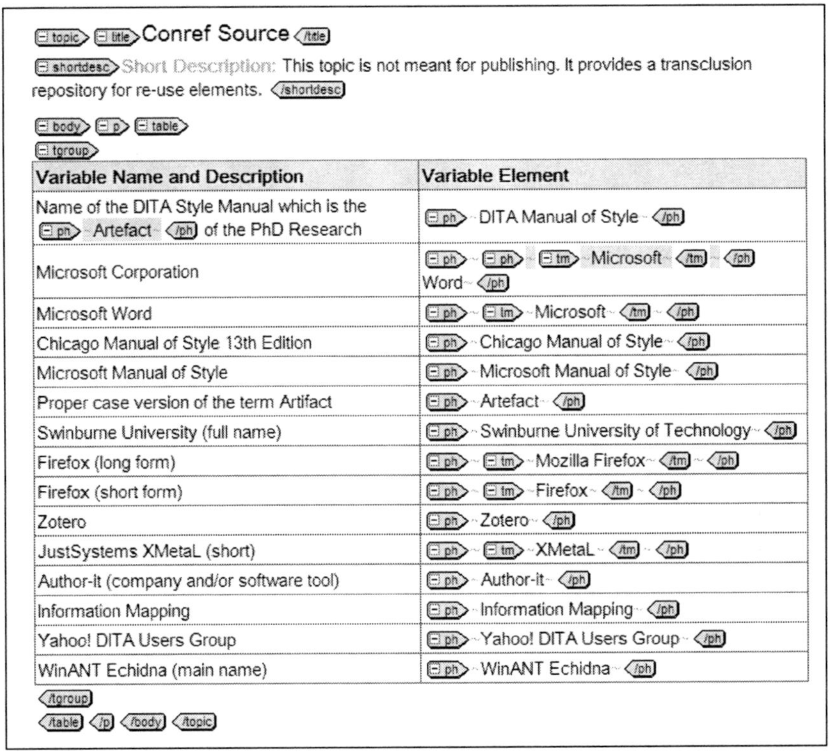

<topic> <title>Conref Source</title>

<shortdesc>Short Description: This topic is not meant for publishing. It provides a transclusion repository for re-use elements. </shortdesc>

<body> <p> <table>
<tgroup>

Variable Name and Description	Variable Element
Name of the DITA Style Manual which is the <ph> Artefact </ph> of the PhD Research	<ph> DITA Manual of Style </ph>
Microsoft Corporation	<ph> <ph> <tm> Microsoft </tm> </ph> Word </ph>
Microsoft Word	<ph> <tm> Microsoft </tm> </ph>
Chicago Manual of Style 13th Edition	<ph> Chicago Manual of Style </ph>
Microsoft Manual of Style	<ph> Microsoft Manual of Style </ph>
Proper case version of the term Artifact	<ph> Artefact </ph>
Swinburne University (full name)	<ph> Swinburne University of Technology </ph>
Firefox (long form)	<ph> <tm> Mozilla Firefox </tm> </ph>
Firefox (short form)	<ph> <tm> Firefox </tm> </ph>
Zotero	<ph> Zotero </ph>
JustSystems XMetaL (short)	<ph> <tm> XMetaL </tm> </ph>
Author-it (company and/or software tool)	<ph> Author-it </ph>
Information Mapping	<ph> Information Mapping </ph>
Yahoo! DITA Users Group	<ph> Yahoo! DITA Users Group </ph>
WinANT Echidna (main name)	<ph> WinANT Echidna </ph>

</tgroup>
</table> </p> </body> </topic>

Finding elements to re-use

One of the challenges of working with re-use elements is how to find and otherwise manage them.

The questions that content authors encounter include:

- How do I know whether I have previously written something that I need to re-use?
- If I know I've already written something on this subject, but where did I write that?
- If I have a chunk of information that I know will be common to three similar tasks, which task do I put the "master" one in?
- Can I have conrefs that conref other chunks? Or is that crazy?

Using centralized files to store re-use elements is one strategy that partly helps to resolve these questions. Using logical names for re-use elements is another. However, DITA-aware *Content Management Systems* have built-in tools for finding re-use opportunities and maintaining re-use elements.

Embedded topics and ditamaps

It is possible to create a *document* made up of one topic. For example, you may be writing a product information sheet as a reference topic type, and that's it. The sheet doesn't belong in a manual or in a collection of topics. It's a standalone topic. However, this scenario is the exception, rather than the rule.

The purpose of a ditamap is to *bind* a set of topics together into a *collection*, using topic reference (`topicref`) elements. The same topic can be re-used in different ditamaps defining different output publications.

There is another way in which you can collect topics together: through a *ditabase* topic. It's not necessarily the right way to collect topics, but it may be appropriate in some circumstances (although some DITA purists would say that it is never appropriate). The *ditabase* information type was designed as a means of collecting multiple topics together into one composite file.

The root node of a *ditabase* topic is `dita`. The `dita` element (or *wrapper*) allows you to nest several *child* topics (as siblings of each other). You can mix and match topic types in this way, such that a `dita` element could contain three `task` elements, a `concept` element, two `topic` elements, and a `reference` element.

If constituent topics are transcluded into the composite *ditabase* topic, those topics can be re-used in other composite topics. In other words, the *ditabase* topic can serve as an alternative to a ditamap.

You should avoid or at least minimize the technique, though. Topics embedded in other topics become difficult to re-use, and difficult to handle in other ways.

The preferred method of re-using topics is with the ditamap.

Advanced conref principles

The features and capabilities of content referencing was extended in DITA 1.2, making it possible to conref multiple elements at the one time, to indirectly reference content, and to *push* content from the source element.

Transcluding a group of elements as a whole

When you need to *conref* a series or sequence of elements in a structure like a set of steps, there is no parent structure to reference. For example, if the first three steps of the following sequence were to be re-used, there doesn't seem to be a structure to group just those three steps and not the following two.

```
<task id="proc">
...
 <steps>
   <step><cmd id="A">Do this.</step>
   <step><cmd id="B">Then do that.</cmd></step>
   <step><cmd id="C">Do the other.</cmd></step>
   <step><cmd id="D">Do something different.</cmd></
step>
   <step><cmd id="E">Then do something else.</cmd></
step>
 </steps>
...
</task>
```

The only obvious approach is to reference step elements A, B and C individually.

However, in DITA 1.2, the *conref* feature was enhanced to make this sort of construct possible. The new attribute which enables the feature is the `conrefend` attribute. You use the standard `conref` attribute to use that attribute to specify the `id` of the element at the start of the group of elements, and the `conrefend` attribute to specify the `id` of the last element in the group of elements. If a `conrefend` attribute is not specified, the conref behaves as a standard, single element transclusion.

To re-use the first three steps in the preceding steps block example, and add a different fourth step, the code would be:

```
<steps>
  <step conref="abc.dita#proc/A"
conrefend="abc.dita#proc/C"><cmd/></step>
  <step><cmd>Do something entirely new.</cmd></step>
</steps>
```

The content block has to be referenced at the step level, not at the `cmd` level, because the elements have to be adjacent (that is, *siblings*).

Note: You could alternatively use the `bodyDiv` element introduced in DITA 1.2 to group a set of elements into a single element, and then transclude the `bodyDiv` element as required.

Indirect content referencing

You may sometimes need to conref different text depending upon the context of the output publication. For example, when publishing a user guide for the Australian market you may want to include the telephone number of the Australian office, but when publishing for the New Zealand market you may want to include the New Zealand office number. You could use conditional publishing in this scenario, but the keyref feature is much simpler.

The process is to use a `conkeyref` attribute to reference a key to the topic containing the re-use elements, and the `id` attribute of the element to re-use, using the syntax *`key/id`*.

For example, instead of `<ph conref="conref_contacts.dita#contacts/aus_phone" />`, you would use the code `<ph conkeyref="reuse/office_phone" />`. In the Australian user guide ditamap, you would define the URI of the topic with a key of `reuse` in the Australian context, such as `<topicref keys="reuse" href="reuse_aus.dita"/>`. In the New Zealand user guide ditamap, you could define the `reuse` key as `<topicref keys="reuse" href="reuse_nz.dita"/>`. Both topics would have a phrase (`ph`) element with an `id` of `office_phone`, containing the respective telephone numbers.

The conref push technique

The normal method of using content references is to reference, in the `conref` attribute of an element in a topic, the element in a source file that you want to re-use, and *pull in* that element's value.

In DITA 1.2, an alternative method of content referencing was introduced, allowing the value of an element to be *pushed*, or injected, from the source element into a topic where it is to be re-used. This technique is known as *conref push*.

A scenario in which *conref push* would be useful would be where a car manufacturer produces driver manuals that are customized by the local car dealer before printing. The customization might simply involve inserting paragraphs with local contact details. The dealer would not want to modify the manufacturer-supplied content, because otherwise those changes would have to be repeated when the manufacturer modified the content.

The conref push mechanism requires elements in the target topic (the topic where the content is to be *pushed*) having id elements, as the push mechanism inserts elements before or after a named element, or replaces the named element.

For example, there might be a need to insert dealer contact details between these two paragraphs:

```
<p id="regular_servicing">You should have your car
serviced regularly.</p>
<p>The service intervals...</p>
```

The paragraph to be *injected* would be maintained in the topic where conref source elements are stored. To *push* the paragraph, a `conref` attribute and a `conaction` attributes must be specified; the `conref` attribute is a reference to the point in the target topic where the content is to be pushed, and the `conaction` nominates whether the element is injected before, after, or replaces the referenced element. If the conref source topic is included within a ditamap, the conref push will be processed during publishing of that ditamap.

To confirm that the topic will be valid after the element is pushed, actions that inject content before or after an element require a “dummy” placeholder element of the same type as the referenced element in the conref source topic.

For example, a new paragraph would be inserted after the `regular_servicing` paragraph with the following code in the conref source topic:

```
<p conaction="mark" conref="c_servicing.dita#service/
regular_servicing" />
<p conaction="pushafter">
  Your local dealer is Snell Performance Vehicles.
</p>
```

To insert a new paragraph before the `regular_servicing` paragraph, the following code would be used:

```
<p conaction="pushbefore">
  You can have your car serviced at Snell
Performance Vehicles, your local dealer.
</p>
<p conaction="mark" conref="c_servicing.dita#service/
regular_servicing" />
```

To replace the `regular_servicing` paragraph, the following code would be used:

```
<p conaction="pushreplace"
conref="c_servicing.dita#service/regular_servicing">
  You should have your car serviced regularly by
Snell Performance Vehicles.
</p>
```

The valid values for the `conaction` attribute are:

pushreplace replaces the referenced element with the re-use element

pushbefore injects the re-use element after the referenced element

pushafter injects the re-use element before the referenced element

mark used as a placeholder in the re-use topic when pushbefore or pushafter actions are used

Chapter 8: Metadata, conditional processing, and indexing

What's in this chapter?

- Conditional processing concepts
- Condition (or select) attributes
- Filtering and flagging
- Other metadata
- Indexing

> Knowledge is not gained by collecting information, but by understanding what information to throw away.
>
> **John Durham Peters**

Conditional processing concepts

Conditional publishing or *conditional processing* in DITA is the technique where metadata attributes set in the DITA content are used as the basis for *filtering* (excluding) or *flagging* (highlighting) portions of the content during the transformation process. The rules for what to filter or flag are typically defined in a separate *DITA values* (*ditaval*) file, which is nominated when the transformation process is started.

Flagging is a method of highlighting where the content is highlighted with a symbol or formatting. The rules for flagging are typically defined in the *ditaval* file.

Nearly all DITA elements, from topics through to inline elements, have a common set of metadata attributes intended for conditional processing:

- audience
- platform
- product
- otherprops

For example, a paragraph in a topic might have an `audience` attribute of `administrator`, and in some contexts, the content needs be published so that any administrator paragraphs are excluded. In this case, the *ditaval* file would be defined so that elements with an audience attribute value of administrator are excluded.

The rev attribute, also common to most DITA elements, can be used for flagging, but not filtering. It is used for recording the version or revision of the documentation in which the element was added or changed.

Condition (or *select*) attributes

The metadata attributes used for conditional publishing through filtering and flagging are audience, platform, product, and otherprops. The rev attribute can be used for flagging only, but not for filtering (excluding). These attributes are sometimes collectively referred to as *condition attributes*, or *select attributes*.

The attribute values are free-form text, although in DITA 1.2, the subjectScheme feature can be used to define a list of controlled values for different attributes.

Attributes can contain multiple values; these are delimited with a space. Values are case-sensitive.

The audience attribute is designed to identify the intended audience of the content. Examples of possible values include administrator, novice, power, Canada, driver, and engineer.

The platform attribute is designed to identify the operating system or other technology platform that the content is specific to. Examples of possible values include macos, linux, firefox, mobile, 4WD, android and ipad.

The product attribute is designed to identify the product that the content is specific to. Examples of possible values include ej25, lite, pro, SR71, acme, STi, and openoffice.

The otherprops attribute is designed to identify any other metadata category to be used as a basis for filtering or flagging. Examples of otherprops use include to identify markets (eg, healthcare), publications (eg, NewsToday), organizational departments (eg, accountspayable), and outlet (eg, melbourne_retail).

Attributes with multiple values

In many cases, you may want to apply more than one value to a metadata attribute. For example, a paragraph may relate to audiences of both `admin` and `manager`.

Attributes can take more than one value. Spaces are used as *delimiters*, to separate the different values. For example, a paragraph with two audience values would be marked up as:

```
<p audience="admin manager">The installation...</p>
```

Obviously, then, individual values of metadata attributes must not contain spaces.

Controlled values for attributes

DITA 1.2 introduced the ability for the author to specify a set of valid metadata attribute values in the ditamap, and have the authoring tool validate the topics to ensure only listed attribute values were used.

The valid attribute values are stored in a `subjectScheme` section in the ditamap.

You should store the `subjectScheme` in a nested ditamap. This is because `subjectScheme` sections are likely to be re-used, and having separate files makes for easier organization.

This sample mark-up shows controlled values for the `platform` attribute of linux, mswin, and zos:

```
<subjectScheme>
  <subjectdef keys="os" navtitle="Operating system">
    <subjectdef keys="linux" navtitle="Linux"/>
    <subjectdef keys="mswin" navtitle="Microsoft
Windows"/>
    <subjectdef keys="zos" navtitle="z/OS"/>
  </subjectdef>
  <enumerationdef>
    <attributedef name="platform"/>
    <subjectdef keyref="os"/>
  </enumerationdef>
</subjectScheme>
```

Conventions for the `otherprops` attribute

The `otherprops` attribute can be used for storing any other metadata information that does not otherwise fit into the standard condition attributes (`audience`, `platform`, and `product`).

To extend the functionality of the `otherprops` attribute, a naming convention can be used that a processor can interpret and action. For example, settings of `otherprops="Market(Australia)"` and `otherprops="Publication(Symmetry)"` would allow the same attribute to be used for a number of functions. In this example, a processor could differentiate between “Market” and “Publication”.

The `props` attribute

The `props` attribute is technically one of the select (or condition) attributes, designed for filtering and flagging during publishing. However, the `props` attribute is not intended to be used within a topic or document. It is provided to be used as the basis for specialized condition attributes.

Do not use this attribute when authoring DITA topics or maps.

Filtering and flagging

Excluding topics: conditional processing at topic level

If you want to exclude a topic in a collection from the output, you have a number of options. These include:

- Not including the topic in the ditamap, and processing a different ditamap when the topic is required.
- Setting a condition attribute in the topic so that the topic can be filtered during the build process.
- Setting a condition attribute in the topicref in the ditamap.

The best option is to construct different ditamap files for different publication outputs, rather than try to use the same ditamap with many condition attributes. The effort required to set up and maintain the condition attributes is a lot higher than working with different maps, particularly when the technique of using nested maps is used.

If having separate ditamaps is not practical, the best approach is to filter at the ditamap level (that is, apply the condition attribute value in the `topicref` element). If the topic is also referenced in the reltable section of the map, you must also apply the condition attribute to those `topicref` elements.

If a topic is to be excluded from an output based on conditions, logic suggests that the filtering condition attribute should be applied to the topic root element, and **not** to the `topicref` element (as recommended). For example, if the topic is intended for administrators only, then the condition metadata should be stored in the topic. However, excluding the entire content of a topic would leave an empty XML file; that is, an XML file without a root element. Such a file would be invalid, as an XML file must have a root element! The processing would then have to stop.

Applying a filtering attribute to the `topicref` element in the ditamap will only exclude the topic from the output if there is only the one reference to that topic. You should take care if applying conditions in the topic that you apply the conditions to all references to the topic, and that you do not leave *dangling topicrefs*.

Conditional processing dangers

When using filtering in single-sourcing, you must be careful to ensure that a conditional processing rule doesn't result in invalid DITA. Filtering must not result in a required element being removed during processing.

For example, in the following snippet, if a condition of "exclude web_only and exclude print_only" was set, there would be no steps in the task, and the topic would be invalid. (The `steps` element requires at least one child `step` element.)

```
<task id="myTopic">
<title>Making a Warranty Claim</title>
<taskbody>
<context>...</context>
   <steps>
  <step otherprops="web_only">...</step>
  <step otherprops="print_only">...</step>
</steps>
<result>...</result>
```

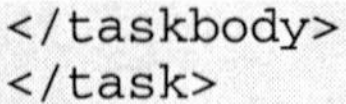

```
</taskbody>
</task>
```

Conditions versus transclusion

There are single-source publishing scenarios where a desired result can be achieved with either conditional processing or with transclusion (the *conref* feature).

For example, if a product name was going to vary between two choices from publication to publication, conditional processing with a product attribute could be used to exclude the inappropriate product name (to leave the appropriate product name). The code might look like: <ph product="Liberty">Liberty><ph product="Legend">Legend</ph>. When a ditaval rule of exclude elements with a product attribute of Liberty is applied, the remaining code would be <ph product="Legend">Legend</ph>.

The alternative approach would be to use transclusion, such as through a content reference (*conref*) to achieve the same result. The product name would not be included directly in the text; instead, a conref would be used to draw the phrase in from a separate conref file. The code might look like: <ph conref="conref_source/product_name" />. When a publication for the product with a name of “Legend” is required, the conref source file could be modified so that the conref source code was: <ph id="product_name">Legend</ph>.

The keyref feature introduced in DITA 1.2 makes this second transclusion method a lot easier and cleaner.

There are pros and cons with either approach.

The main advantages of the conditional processing method are:

- all variations are visible to the author
- a review version of the document can be produced that shows all variations

The main advantages of the transclusion method are:

- topics are easier for an author to read
- doesn’t rely on metadata

- easier to maintain if new variations are introduced(only the conref source file needs to be updated)
- can cope better with large numbers of conditions

Include and exclude filtering actions

The *DITA values* (*ditaval*) file is used to specify publishing conditions used for processing DITA source into a reading format. The condition actions are specified in the `action` attribute of the `prop` element in the ditaval file. Valid action are:

exclude exclude from the output any elements with the specified metadata attributes

flag highlight, with a text colour, background colour, or image, any elements with the specified metadata attributes

passthough ignore the attribute, but leave the attribute in place in the output

include include from the output any elements with the specified metadata attributes

An example of a snippet of ditaval code to flag elements with a `product` attribute of `impress` with a small image at the start of the element is:

```
<prop att="product" val="impress" action="flag">
  <startflag imageref="delta_olive.gif">
    <alt-text>Start of product - Impress</alt-text>
  </startflag>
</prop>
```

Despite there being an include action in the ditaval logic, there is no purpose for this action. By default, **all** content is included. Even within a nested set of elements, a higher level element marked as include will have no affect even if lower level elements are marked with exclude. By default, no content is flagged.

Attributes are used to mark elements that are specific or individual to a particular product, platform, audience or other requirement. You only mark up those elements that you want the ability to exclude or flag.

If you are using multiple conditions (that is, more than one value in the same attribute, such as `audience="admin manager"`), if any exclude condition is satisfied, then the element will be excluded from the output.

So if a paragraph was marked with values of `admin` and `manager`, and the ditaval specified that `admin` should be excluded, but `manager` included, the paragraph would be excluded.

Limiting the use of conditions

In traditional publishing processes, *conditions* or *build tags* set on document elements have been a key enabler of conditional publishing. Technical communicators working with tools such as FrameMaker and RoboHelp sometimes create complicated nested conditions, so that numerous permutations of a document can be produced from the one project. In a DITA authoring environment, which is modular and library-focused rather than document-focused, there are additional, more flexible, mechanisms for single-sourcing.

In a DITA environment, there should be greater focus on writing more *agnostically*, so that complicated conditions are not necessary. DITA encourages more information analysis than earlier approaches to documentation, and during that analysis, authors should investigate whether context-agnostic writing may be a better approach than very context-specific writing where conditions become overly important.

For example, if a topic includes a product name, which may vary from publication to publication, you may be able to phrase your content so that the specific product name is not used.

Filtering ditamaps

It is possible in DITA, and often good practice, to have nested ditamaps. Although it does depend on circumstance, it is generally better practice to apply conditions to the `topicref` or `mapref` element, rather than the `map` element of the nested ditamap.

The reason for this, and a point that should always be considered when deciding on a filtering strategy, is the reduced processing load during generation of the output. If the processor has to read in a topic, or a nested map, only to find it's not needed in the current build because of the filtering metadata, it is an inefficient model. It is much better for the exclusion to be notified to the processor before having to load the file.

Filtering composite (*ditabase*) topics

Although you should avoid the use of composite topics in any case, there are some complications when filtering such content.

If you have a ditamap `topicref` element with a condition attribute pointing to a topic within a composite topic file, then excluding elements with that attribute in the build process will not result in the (nested) topic being excluded from the output, unless that (nested) topic also has the condition attribute. The processor will include the entire composite topic if any topic within that composite topic is included in the published output.

Even if the chunking feature is used to split the composite DITA topic into multiple HTML topics, for example, the entire contents of the DITA topic will be output unless condition attributes are applied within the topic.

Print versus non-print metadata

There are a number of ways of differentiating "Web-only" and "print-only" content, or other medium-dependent conditions. The best method will depend on the semantics involved, and the particular scenario.

In many cases, marking up content using `otherprops` attribute values of, for example, `manual_only` and `web_only` may be appropriate. If the reason for the differentiation relates to the different audiences for print and Web deliverables, then the audience attribute would be a better choice. In the same way, if the reason for differentiation was that you are producing two separate document products, such as a book to be sold on the Web and a book to be sold in bookshops, the `product` attribute is more suitable.

The `topicref` element in the ditamap has a `print` attribute with valid values of yes and no. If you are simply wanting to exclude complete topics from the print version of a document, this attribute should be used.

If you have some common and some different topics for print and Web versions, you may find that creating two ditamaps, one for print and one for Web, is a better approach than applying conditions to the `topicref` elements in a single ditamap.

Other metadata

Managing metadata elements and attributes

When working in a topic-based, modular architecture, where metadata plays a key role, one of the major challenges for authors is managing metadata. In this respect, "managing metadata" means such things as ensuring consistent metadata use, using metadata for retrieval of authoring topics, enforcing business metadata rules, and effective use of conditional metadata attributes. The most effective way of managing metadata is through a *Content Management System* (*CMS*).

If a *CMS* is not being used, you may find that recording metadata attribute values used in a collection inside a comments area within the ditamap XML code might be helpful.

There are some DITA software tools that provide some features that leverage metadata, such as reporting on attribute values in a collection. You may find these tools useful in supplementing your authoring tool features. Two such tools are DITAinformationcenter and WinANT Echidna.

Critical dates

The topic's `prolog` element (and the `topicmeta` equivalent in the ditamap) contains a `critdates` element, which is used to store date information relating to the document life cycle. Two types of date information can be stored in specific date elements:

`created` element	dates associated with the topic as originally created
`revised` element	dates associated with the most recently revised content in the topic

Only one `created` element is allowed, but as many `revised` elements as required are allowed.

The `created` element can store specific dates in the following attributes:

date	the topic creation date

golive the date the topic was released (made generally available)

expiry the date when the topic content is expected to become obsolete (or need to be reviewed)

The `revised` element can store specific dates in the following attributes:

modified the date the content of the topic was last modified

golive the date the modified topic was released (made generally available)

expiry the date when the topic content is expected to become obsolete (or need to be reviewed)

All dates should be entered in *YYYY-MM-DD* format, where *YYYY* is the year, *MM* is the number of the month, and *DD* is the number of the day.

An example of a `critdates` section is:

```
<critdates>
  <created date="2009-10-22" golive="2009-11-30" />
  <revised modified="2009-12-01" golive="2010-01-01"
expiry="2010-02-27" />
  <revised modified="2010-02-09" golive="2010-02-27"
expiry="2010-12-30" />
</critdates>
```

Author, publisher and publication metadata

Publications, and individual topics, can have publication metadata associated with them. This metadata includes:

- the name of the author (or authors)
- the name of the publisher
- the name of the copyright holder
- the product the information relates to

This metadata is stored in a number of elements within the `topicmeta` section of a ditamap, and in the equivalent `prolog` section of a topic.

The `author` element contains the name of the document or topic author, and can be used as many times as required. It stores additional information about the author in the following attributes:

href contains the URL of the author's e-mail address or Web site, or the address of a DITA topic in the collection containing information about the author

type allows the role of the author to be specified, with values of creator (primary author) and contributor (for contributing author).

The `publisher` element contains the name of the document publisher, and is only allowed to be used once. It stores additional information about the publisher in the following attribute:

href contains the URL of the publisher's e-mail address or Web site, or the address of a DITA topic in the collection containing information about the publisher

The `copyright` element doesn't contain text; it only stores information in nested elements and attributes. The copyright element can be used as many times as required (to cater for joint copyright ownership of a work). If there **is** more than one copyright holder, the `type` attribute can be used to nominate whether the holder is the primary holder or the secondary holder. The `copyright` element has two nested elements: `copyryear` (which is mandatory) and `copyrholder`.

The `copyryear` element doesn't contain text, and only contains one `year` attribute. You should enter the year of copyright in this attribute, in *YYYY* format. More than one `copyryear` element can be included within a copyright element if the copyright extends over more than one year.

The `copyrholder` element simply contains the legal name of the copyright holder.

The `prodinfo` element contains information about the product (or products) that are the subject matter of the publication or topic. The `prodinfo` element doesn't contain text; instead, it contains the following elements:

`prodname` element	the name of the product that is the subject matter

`vrmlist` element	itself contains a series of `vrm` elements that contain the version, release and modification information about the product
`brand` element	the manufacturer or brand associated with the product
`series` element	the product series that the product belongs to
`platform` element	if the product is a software product, the platform or operating system that the product runs on
`prognum` element	the product code, program number, order number or other identifying number used for the product
`featnum` element	most relevant to the topic prolog, rather than map topicmeta, this is the internal feature number or other identifier
`component` element	the component of the product that this topic relates to

An example of a `topicmeta` section containing some of these elements is:

```
<topicmeta>
  <author href="mailto:leo@smiggins.com">Leo
Smiggins</author>
  <publisher>FJ Heavy Industries</publisher>
  <copyright>
    <copyryear year="2009"></copyryear>
    <copyrholder>Supara Australia</copyrholder>
  </copyright>
  <prodinfo>
    <prodname>Impress XRW</prodname>
    <brand>Supara</brand>
    <series>Impress</series>
  </prodinfo>
</topicmeta>
```

The `outputclass` attribute

Most block and phrase elements in DITA have an `outputclass` attribute. This attribute is used to provide output styling information, when necessary.

When published to an HTML-based output format, the value in the `outputclass` attribute of an element will be passed through to the CSS `class` attribute in the HTML code.

You should avoid using the `outputclass` attribute, as it is not a semantic marker. The presentation of the output should be determined by the publishing tool automatically converting semantic mark-up to formatting rules.

The `status` attribute

Most DITA content elements include the `status` attribute. This attribute makes most sense when applied to the top-level topic element, such as `concept`, `task` and `reference` elements, and you can use it to record the status or progress of the information in its life cycle.

Valid values for the `status` attribute are:

- new
- changed
- deleted
- unchanged

Some authoring tools may highlight topics with different `status` attribute values in different ways, and some publishing tools may also take advantage of the attribute values.

The `importance` attribute

Most DITA content elements include the `importance` attribute. You can use this attribute to indicate the relative importance of an element, such as a step, in its broader context.

Valid values for the importance attribute are:

- obsolete
- deprecated
- optional
- default
- low
- normal
- high

- recommended
- required
- urgent

Some publishing tools may highlight elements with a higher priority in some way. For example, in a task topic, `link` elements (in the `related-links` section) marked with an `importance` attribute value of required will be rendered in the pre-requisites section in the output.

The `source` element

The `source` element in the topic `prolog` section is used to nominate the name and/or location of information from which the topic was drawn or based. It is based on the Dublin Core Metadata Initiative source property. The location of the resource is recorded in the `source` element's `href` attribute.

For example, if a topic was based on figures published in a Department of Transport report, the source element may be coded as:

```
<source href="http://www.transport.gov.au/design/
adr_online.aspx">
  Australian Design Rules
</source>
```

When published to an HTML-based output format, the address in the `href` attribute of the `source` element are included in the Dublin Core `DC.source` metadata in the head section of the HTML page.

Indexing

The indexing features in DITA are built around three elements: `indexterm`, `index-see`, and `index-see-also`. These elements can technically be placed at almost any point in the body of a topic, as well as in the topic `prolog` and in the `topicmeta` of the topicref in the ditamap. However, to avoid potential translation and processing complications, the elements should be deliberately placed in specific locations within the topic or map.

Placement of `indexterm` elements

The alphabetical index of a publication is derived, during the publishing process, from index keyword terms placed by the author throughout topics in the document. Index keyword terms are defined through the `indexterm` element.

DITA allows `indexterm` elements to be placed in:

- the `topicref` in the ditamap
- the `prolog` in the topic
- the `shortdesc` (and `abstract`) in the topic
- the `body` of the topic

However, having index entries scattered throughout the text creates maintenance problems, and may lead to difficulties in translation and processing.

Where possible, `indexterm` elements should be placed in the topic `prolog` section, outside the body of the topic content. In the `prolog`, index entries must be contained within a `keywords` element.

When specific to a publication (and therefore not always applicable to the topic), the `indexterm` elements should be placed in the `topicmeta` section within the `topicref` element in the ditamap. An example of this may be a term that is used by one organization but not others, where different ditamaps define output for different organizations.

Index terms should only be placed within the body text where topics are relatively long. In such cases, index entries in the output might otherwise point to the start of a section of content, rather than the point at which the term is mentioned.

When you need to place the index entry within the body of a topic, follow these placement guidelines:

- for block-level (paragraph) elements: immediately following the start tag of the containing element
- at sentence level: immediately preceding the sentence
- at word or phrase level: immediately preceding the text

> **Note:** The contents of `indexterm` elements are never rendered in the output, including when the `indexterm` elements are inline within the body of the content. Thus, the mark-up: `<p>The EJ25 <indexterm>turborcharger</indexterm> forced`

`induction...</p>` will render as `The EJ25 forced induction....`

In some cases, you may feel you want to use an `indexterm` at a particular point in the document where `indexterm` is not allowed. Although you may be able to technically work around the problem by inserting a phrase (`ph`) element and then inserting the `indexterm` element is the `ph` element, do not do this. Only insert an index term where the element is valid.

Nesting index entries

You can created multi-level (*secondary* and *tertiary*) indexes by nesting `indexterm` elements.

For example, the mark-up:

```
<indexterm>EJ25 engine
  <indexterm>performance</indexterm>
</indexterm>
```

may produce, in a page layout output, and index entry of:

EJ25 engine
    performance 15

The page reference is applied to the innermost term (in the example, "performance") only.

An example of a more complex index result is:

EJ25 engine
    dimensions 72
    maintenance 33
    performance 15
    specifications 49

In a hypertext document that supports multi-level indexes, the same example might be displayed as:

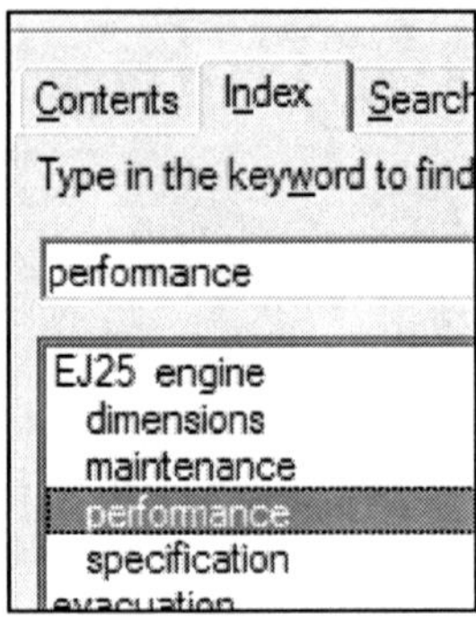

You should avoid nesting index entries to more than three levels. In most cases, one or two levels will provide sufficient scope for a comprehensive and easy-to-navigate index.

If you have a number of secondary entries belonging to the same parent entry, such as "EJ25 engine, performance" and "EJ25 engine, torque", the secondary entries can either be nested under the same parent entry, or structured separately.

In other words,

```
<indexterm>EJ25 engine
  <indexterm>performance</indexterm>
  <indexterm>torque</indexterm>
</indexterm>
```

is equivalent to

```
<indexterm>EJ25 engine
  <indexterm>performance</indexterm>
</indexterm>
<indexterm>EJ25 engine
  <indexterm>torque</indexterm>
</indexterm>
```

Index see and see also

The `index-see` element is used to redirect the reader to a synonymous index term. The `index-see` element is nested inside a standard `indexterm` element, with `indexterm` containing the term to appear in the index, and the `index-see` containing the term for readers to be pointed to. The `index-see` must be the only child element of the parent `indexterm`.

For example, the code

```
<indexterm>forced induction
   <index-see>turbocharger</index-see>
</indexentry>
```

will result in an output of:

forced induction, See turbocharger

Where possible, index-see entries should be placed in the ditamap topicmeta, because they are logically applicable at the publication level, rather than the topic level.

The structure of the index-see entry in the ditamap is shown in the example:

```
<map id="lumberer_om_05">
  <title>Lumberer XT Owner's Manual</title>
  <topicmeta>
    <keywords>
      <indexterm>forced induction
        <index-see>turbocharger</index-see>
      </indexterm>
    </keywords>
  </topicmeta>
  <topicref...>...</topicref>
  <topicref...>...</topicref>
  <topicref...>...</topicref>
        ...
</map>
```

The index-see-also element is similar in function to index-see, except that it also provides a page reference to the original term.

For example, the code

```
<indexterm>forced induction
   <index-see-also>turbocharger</index-see-also>
</indexentry>
```

will result in an output of:

forced induction 15
    See turbocharger

Do not use index-see-also in the ditamap top level map element's topicmeta, although you can use it within the topicref element's topicmeta within the ditamap.

In a hypertext document that supports indexes, the same example might be displayed as:

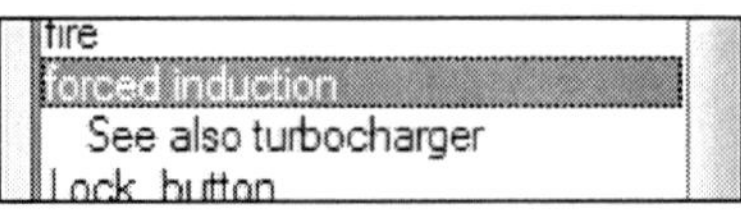

Re-using index entries

Like most DITA elements, index elements can be re-used through the *conref* mechanism. There are good reasons why you might want to re-use index entries, including consistency of wording and punctuation, and reduced translation costs. (Even if used in more than one place, re-used index entries only have to be translated once in the conref source.)

You may find that you can better manage the re-use of index terms if they are stored in their own, standalone, ditamap. That index re-use ditamap will never be processed, and never embedded in another ditamap; it is only used for the purposes of re-use. Such a ditamap file should be named with a prefix of `conref_source_`. The ditamap could easily be used by many authors working in the same team.

The code for an index re-use ditamap would follow the pattern:

```
<map id="conref_index_reuse">
  <title>Index Term Re-use</title>
  <topicmeta>
    <keywords>
      <indexterm
id="index_turbocharger">turbocharger</indexterm>
      <indexterm id="index_keypad_PIN">keypad
        <indexterm>PIN</indexterm>
      </indexterm>
      <indexterm id="index_immobiliser">immobiliser</
indexterm>
      ...
    </keywords>
  </topicmeta>
</map>
```

Chapter 9: The DITA documentation process

What's in this chapter?

- Structured authoring documentation stages
- Unit testing in a team
- Restricting authors and limiting element choices
- File and folder naming conventions
- Elements for pre-publish review
- The DITA publishing process
- Page numbering in page layout documents
- Content Management Systems

> The most difficult thing is the decision to act, the rest is merely tenacity. The fears are paper tigers. You can do anything you decide to do. You can act to change and control your life; and the procedure, the process is its own reward.
>
> **Amelia Earhart**

Structured authoring documentation stages

The process of creating, producing and delivering a document in DITA's modular, structured authoring environment can be divided into three different stages:

Building Building is the authoring process, normally undertaken by a writer.

Associating Associating is the drawing together of the topics into collections (such as books and Web sites), normally undertaken by the *information architects*. A bundle of independent topics only becomes a book when the topics are associated, or linked, to each other through the ditamap.

Publishing Publishing is the generation of the output collections of topics. The output might be a Word document, a PDF document, a CHM file, a collection of HTML files, or even a collection of XML files.

Note: Building and associating are independent, and are not sequential stages.

Unit testing in a team

When a team of authors is working on the same collection of topics, particularly when the collection is very large, it is sometimes difficult to identify a problem with the build. For example, a topic referenced in the *master* ditamap may be invalid; finding that invalid topic in a large collection will be difficult.

Some information architects provide each author with a ditamap of that author's topics. Before the author submits the final set of topics, the ditamap must successfully and cleanly build as a unit. The author's ditamap can be discarded after testing if it is not otherwise used for publishing.

This unit testing approach allows any issues to be addressed in a smaller, quicker to build, environment.

Restricting authors and limiting element choices

Some authoring teams choose to restrict the DITA elements they allow their authors to use. This might be an informal restriction ("don't do it or else!"), or a formal restriction (by software).

Some DITA authoring tools provide the facility to restrict or limit the elements displayed in the authoring interface. The restrictions are usually managed on the basis of element mark-up domains, which are groups of elements intended for common subject matter.

Figure 43: Example of an authoring tool dialog box for hiding DITA mark-up domains

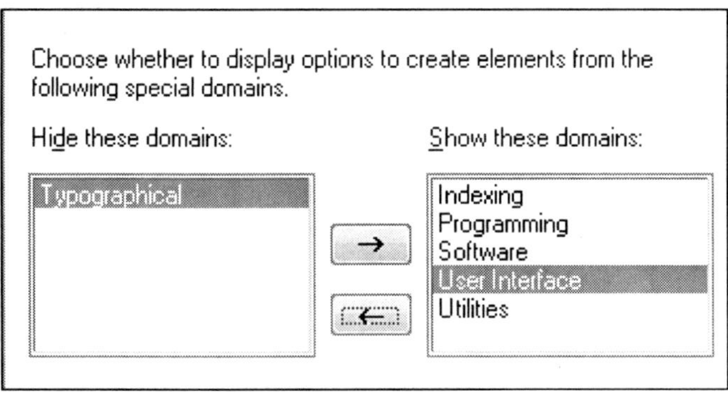

The *constraints* mechanism introduced in DITA 1.2 provides a standard for creating constrained information types, which can be used to make the element choices for the author simpler.

File and folder naming conventions

Use descriptive folder and file names. Use `.dita` as the file extension for topic files, and `.ditamap` for ditamap files. File names are case-sensitive, and lower case file names are preferred. Prefix topic names with a letter corresponding to their information type.

File and folder structure

The ideal file structure for a DITA project is to have ditamaps at the root level of the documentation repository folder, and content topics stored in sub-folders down from the root. This structure ensures that *topicref* links to content always move down the tree structure. As ditamaps are an informational superset of topics, having ditamaps in a *superfolder* is a logical approach.

Images and other media resources should be stored in a separate folder (eg, `/images`).

There are a number of file topologies that you can use, including:

- by information type (eg, concept, task, reference)
- by system component documented (eg, engine, fuel system)
- by subject area (eg, Getting Started, Working with Debits).

Using a logical, context-free storage location for topics reduces the problems associated with having to later move files from one project folder to another project folder. It also makes the files easier to find.

Never base storage locations on where you want to output files to be generated, as this introduces context into file locations, and breaks the fundamental principle of separation of content from format from delivery.

Avoid using a *flat* or *shallow* file structure, with hundreds of topic files stored in one folder. This structure may result in slower file retrieval in DITA editors, where the **File Open** dialog, for instance, needs to list all the files for selection.

File names

When choosing file names, observe the following guidelines.

- Use descriptive, short names, in lower case.
- Use alphanumeric characters.
- Prefer complete words to abbreviations.
- Do not use spaces (use underscores rather than spaces between words).
- Prefix the file name with a character identifying the information type (`c`, `t`, `r`), separated by an underscore character.
- Be consistent.

An example of a file name for a task topic with a title of "Refreshing the cache" is: `t_refreshing_the_cache.dita`

The use of descriptive names and underscore separators aims to enhance human readability and identification.

Case-sensitive file and folder names

Even though some tools and environments may be case-insensitive when it comes to file and folder names, you must be totally consistent with the case of your file and folder names. One important aspect of DITA is interchangeability, and if you are not consistent with file name case, your documents may cause problems when you interchange with someone in a case-sensitive environment.

Further, some DITA tools treat file names differently within the same workflow (or *pipeline*). For example, one part of the DITA Open Toolkit pipeline checks with the operating system to see if a file (`abc.dita`) exists before proceeding to the next step. The operating system may respond `yes` if a file named `ABC.dita` exists, even though a file name of the exact case (`abc.dita`) does not exist. When the next step (which is *case aware*) commences, it may crash because it cannot find a file `abc.dita`.

Treat file and folder names as case-sensitive.

Avoiding special characters in file names

Using special characters in file names may cause some problems or errors in some authoring and publishing tools. Special characters in this context means symbols, typographical characters, punctuation characters, spaces, diacritical characters, and non-Latin characters.

You should treat file names as though they are URIs, and follow the IETF syntax conventions for URI naming.

Refer to IETF Uniform Resource Identifier (URI): Generic Syntax for the comprehensive URI guidelines.

File extensions for DITA topics and ditamaps

Most DITA authoring tools allow you to save topics with `.dita` or `.xml` file extensions.

Always use the `.dita` file extension.

The reasons for using `.dita` extensions include:

- DITA authoring tools can be associated specifically with DITA topics. A generic `.xml` file name doesn't identify the file sufficiently - it could be a DITA file or an XML file of any other type. For example, using the `.dita` extension would allow you to configure Windows so that double-clicking the file opens it in your preferred DITA editor.
- It is easier for you to recognise DITA files when browsing folders by the unique `.dita` file extension.
- Within a DITA process, there are XML file formats other than DITA topics and ditamaps. For example, there are XML build files and ditaval files. Using `.dita` for topics helps differentiate topics from other supporting files.

Most authoring tools also allow you to save ditamap files with a `.ditamap` extension or a `.xml` extension.

Always use the `.ditamap` extension for all ditamap files, including bookmaps.

Specialized element and attribute naming convention

When the DITA schema is specialized to suit a particular documentation purpose, the person creating the specialization (the *specializer*) must choose names for elements and attributes.

It is technically valid for the *specializer* to use all lower case (`buttonname`), lower case with hyphens (`button-name`), *CamelCase* (`ButtonName`), lower then CamelCase (`buttonName`), or some other permutation. However, *CamelCase* with a lower case first letter is the preferred convention.

You should:

- use an identifying prefix to element names
- use element and attribute names in lower then *CamelCase*

In the previous example, the recommended name would therefore be `hwButtonName`.

You must not use names already used in the base DITA content model.

The use of a prefix will make specialized elements more recognizable, and will avoid the chances of a name clash with base DITA names.

Elements for pre-publish review

In a typical documentation process, incomplete information will often prevent the completion of a topic. To help track and manage the incomplete information, an author can add `draft-comment` phrase elements. The `draft-comment` element is also useful during the peer review and editing stages to leave remarks or suggestions for the author to consider or implement.

The `draft-comment` element has an `author` attribute, used to record the name of the author of the comment. An example of the mark-up is:

```
<p>The MY11 XRW uses an AHA turbocharger.
  <draft-comment author="Leo">
    Check if this changed after product meeting
  </draft-comment>
<p>
```

The `draft-comment` element should not be confused with the `required-cleanup` element. The `required-cleanup` element is intended only for identifying text in imported topics (typically, topics converted from XHTML to DITA) where the mark-up was not cleanly converted. In other words, `required-cleanup` content needs a human author to manually correct the mark-up to preserve the original intent.

Any `draft-comment` content will normally be removed during the publishing process. However, some authoring tools allow `draft-comment` elements to be deliberately included in the output.

The draft-comment element is not allowed in some structures. An alternative is to use standard XML comment special element. Many authoring tools allow the addition of XML comments in the *WYSIOO* editor.

The mark-up of an XML comment is shown in the example:

```
<!-- Check that the last step is required for MY11
model -->
```

The DITA publishing process

DITA content can be published to a range of output reading formats using a number of tools. The publishing tools, or DITA processors, use a number of different technologies.

The majority of processors use two key technologies:

XSL-T to transform DITA into another mark-up language, including HTML and DocBook

XSL-FO an XML formatting language used as an intermediary format when DITA is processed to a page layout format such as PDF and RTF

The processing involves a number of steps that interpret ditamaps, resolve conref transclusion elements, resolve cross-references, apply formatting numbering and labels, and map DITA elements to output format elements.

Figure 44: Overview of typical DITA transformation to PDF shows an overview of the tools and upper-level processes involved in converting DITA to PDF.

Figure 44: Overview of typical DITA transformation to PDF

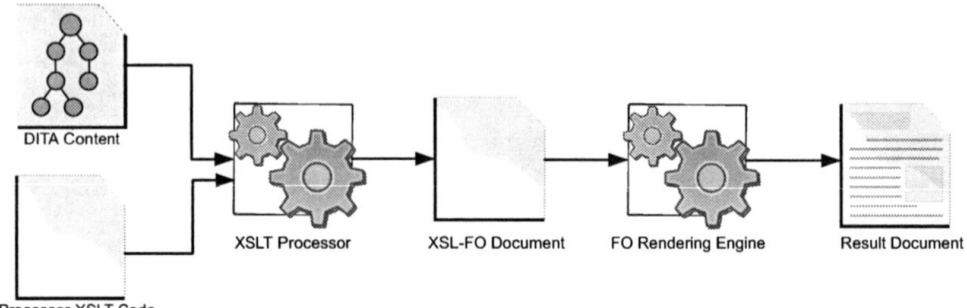

Page numbering in page layout documents

Traditional page numbering systems for printed documents have different numbering ranges for front matter, body content, and back matter. For example, the front matter (such as the Table of Contents, List of Figures, and Acknowledgements) might be numbered in lower case Roman numerals, with the page numbers restarting for the main body content in Arabic numerals.

The historical reasons for the different numbering sequences trace back to the production processes where the Table of Contents couldn't be created until the body of the document was paginated. Technology has since removed that limitation, but in general, the traditional numbering system has persisted.

When creating PDF (or similar page layout) output documents where the intention is that the documents will primarily be read on-screen, you should process the document with a single page numbering sequence. This will make it easier for the document to be navigated, when the actual page numbers in the viewer match the page numbers displayed on the pages in the document.

Content Management Systems

A *Content Management System* (*CMS*) is a software system for managing the documentation development life cycle, including the processes of creating, updating, publishing, and translating information. A *CMS* is particularly important for modular documentation approaches such as DITA, as it allows authors to locate topics or elements already written, manage file and folder naming without breaking cross-referencing and other relationship links, manage content references, allow multiple authors to work collectively on the same documents, and store previous versions of topics for backup, archiving and other version control purposes.

Many systems also allow a *release state* to be used to manage the progression of information from draft, through review, approval and release. Most systems include user rights management, so that different users are given different access to the information according to their role in the documentation process.

In a DITA project, content management is more important if collaboration is required. If one person is responsible for all of the six stages of the content life cycle, the task of managing content is simple. But when there are many authors, many editors, many languages, complicated approval rules, and complicated archival requirements, the management task becomes enormous, and a *CMS* becomes a requirement.

A *CMS* typically supports the following features.

- Import and creation of documents and multimedia material.
- Identification of all key users and their roles.
- The ability to assign roles and responsibilities to different instances of content categories or types.
- The ability to alert interested users to changes in content.

- The ability to track and manage multiple versions of a single instance of content.
- The ability to search through the text or metadata of all content.
- The ability to publish the content.

Content within a DITA *CMS* is normally stored (in DITA format) within a database *repository*. A database makes it easier to manage multiple versions, and retrieve and archive content. Some systems use an XML database, a type of database technology optimized for working with XML files.

Appendix A: DITA authoring concepts

What's in this appendix?

- Introduction to DITA
- Distinction between format and style, and data and metadata
- Specialization
- Generalization
- Constraints

> DITA is an open content standard that defines a common structure for content that promotes the consistent creation, sharing, and reuse of content.
>
> **Ann Rockley**

Introduction to DITA

DITA stands for the Darwin Information Typing Architecture.

The "Darwin" is in homage to Charles Darwin, the famed scientist credited with the theory of evolution following the publication of his *On the Origin of Species*. DITA incorporates principles of specialization, adaption and inheritance that are reminiscent of Darwinian theory (only in a completely different field!).

Figure 45: Charles Darwin

Photo: Library of Congress, Prints & Photographs Division, [reproduction number, LC-USZ61-104]

"Information Type" refers to the focus on categorization of information. (*Typing* means categorization in this context, not keyboarding!)

"Architecture" indicates that DITA is not just an XML standard; it is an approach, a workflow, a methodology, and a philosophy.

One good, short definition of DITA is:

> DITA defines an XML architecture for designing, writing, managing, and publishing many kinds of information in print and on the Web.
>
> **OASIS, DITA XML Cover Pages**

Adopting a DITA approach is not really about tools and technologies. DITA represents a change to the way that information is developed.

History of DITA

DITA was developed by technical communicators, for technical communicators.

DITA started within the technical publications department at IBM. IBM had been using *SGML (Standard Generalized Mark-up Language)* for its documentation for many years, and had pioneered a number of document formats including IBM BookMaster and IBM ID Doc. The knowledge accumulated from working with those document formats was applied to the development of an XML-based document approach. The principal architects of IBM DITA were Don Day, Michael Priestley, and Dave Schell.

DITA became known outside IBM after the publication of *An XML Architecture for Technical Documentation: The Darwin Information Typing Architecture* by Don Day, Erik Hennum, John Hunt, Michael Priestley, and David Schell at the *2003 STC Conference.*

In March 2004, IBM donated DITA to the *OASIS* standards organization, where it is now managed by the *OASIS DITA Technical Committee*, or *DITA TC*. In April 2005, OASIS approved Version 1.0 of the DITA specification. In August 2007, OASIS approved version 1.1 of the DITA specification. In the second half of 2010, version 1.2 of the DITA specification was approved.

The charter of the *DITA TC* is to promote the use of the DITA architecture for creating standard information types and domain-specific mark-up vocabularies. The members of the TC are representatives from different industries, organizations and countries.

The A in DITA

DITA can be described as an approach to information architecture. That's why there's an A for Architecture in DITA!

A great definition of architecture in the DITA context can be found in the book *DITA 101*:

> An open content standard that defines a common structure for content that promotes the consistent creation, sharing, and re-use of content.
>
> **Ann Rockley, Steve Manning, and Charles Cooper**

This definition is great because it highlights the facts that:

- DITA is an open standard
- standards encourage consistency
- consistency allows content re-use and content sharing

OASIS and the DITA Technical Committee

DITA is controlled (or perhaps a better word is "guided") by the *DITA Technical Committee (TC)*. The DITA intellectual property is commonly-owned, with the trustee being OASIS. OASIS is a not-for-profit organization - a standards body. In order to participate in an OASIS TC, including of course the OASIS DITA TC, you must be a member of OASIS. And although OASIS is not-for-profit, it recovers the cost of running the organization through membership fees.

There are a number of membership categories. In brief, it is possible to join as a company or as an individual. *Contributor* company membership has lower annual dues, but *Sponsor* company membership offers more marketing opportunities. A benefits matrix on the OASIS Web site explains the difference between member categories.

Once the company or an individual is an OASIS member, the nominated person is able to participate in any or many OASIS TCs. The DITA TC is getting bigger over time, and doing more and more work. The TC is now spawning sub-committees (SC) to concentrate on more specialized tasks and problems.

Beyond the OASIS membership dues, there are no costs in being involved in TCs and SCs, other than the brainpower and time contributions.

DITA features

DITA's features include:

- modularity
- structured authoring (reduces authoring time, increases analysis time)
- information typing
- minimalism
- inheritance
- specialization
- single-source
- topic-based
- metadata
- conditional processing
- component publishing

- task-orientation
- content re-use
- translation-friendly structure

Information typing

DITA categorizes key business information by communication purpose, or *information type*. There are three base DITA information types: concept, task and reference.

Information typing is also used in other methodologies such as Information Mapping.

Topic-based authoring

DITA has a topic-based architecture, requiring a topic-based approach to document authoring. The term *topic* can be thought of as being short for *topical information unit*, or a *topical unit of discourse*.

A topic-based architecture opens up the opportunity for large scale content re-use. Topics are assembled from a single pool or repository into different deliverable documents. Topics can be used in different publications, provided the topic makes sense when read in different contexts.

A special DITA file called a *map* or *ditamap* is used to specify topics to be included in a deliverable document. The ditamap doesn't store much content; it mainly comprises of pointers to the topics that contain the content.

Not only does a topic-based architecture allow information to be re-used, it also makes translation and localization more efficient because the same information never has to be translated more than once.

Modularity

Modularity is the technique of building large complex things in smaller, self-contained pieces. Modular furniture is a good example of modularity in practice. Instead of being one large piece, a modular couch may be four pieces that can be arranged in different ways to form different couch configurations.

Creation of a manual can also be modularized. Instead of being constructed as one piece, a large manual may be designed as a collection of different modules, and those modules can be arranged into different configurations to create different manuals. Modular manuals are easier to maintain, and can be produced more efficiently. A ditamap referencing a group of topics can be embedded within another ditamap, just as a set of elements within a single topic can be re-used in many different topics.

XML technologies (such as *XPath*) make modularity technically easy to implement. DITA can take advantage of such complementary XML technologies.

Minimalism

Minimalism is an instructional design technique, popularized by John Carroll in his 1990 book *The Nurnberg Funnel: Designing Minimalist Instruction for Practical Computer Skill* . The DITA methodology embraces the concepts of minimalism.

Minimalism is an approach that presents the reader with the smallest amount of information necessary to achieve the reader's goals. The needs of the reader (or the learner), and not the system being documented, guide the information architecture and the writing style.

You can see minimalism principles in particular in the *task* information type (one of the three base information types in DITA), which discourages the inclusion of information not directly related to the procedure by the task topic's strict content model.

For technical documents produced in a DITA environment, design information specifically so that readers only have to read to learn something or to do something.

Structured authoring

The term *structured authoring* is applied to a wide variety of writing approaches, to the point that the meaning is virtually lost. Some say that most technical writing is "structured authoring" or "structured writing", because the writing process is approached in a methodical structured way. According to this definition, all documents with some sort of structure must have been the result of a structured approach.

Methodological or scientific approaches to writing technical documents became prominent in the 1960s, with Robert Horn's structured writing ideas (later to become Information Mapping) and the *STOP* methodology (developed at Hughes-Fullerton) being two of the intellectual products of that era. The development of *SGML* almost two decades later enabled structured approaches to be enforced by software tools. The development of *XML* in the late 1990s transformed the way in which knowledge was stored. XML permitted structured information standards to be created for the storage of knowledge and data for all types of industries. *XML* allowed standards such as *Chemical Mark-up Language, Mathematics Mark-up Language, Channel Definition Format, Scalable Vector Graphics, Open Document Format,* and hundreds of others to be created by industry, government and special interest groups. In the documentation field, new forms of structured writing approaches emerged, enabled by *XML* and the new culture of the open source movement. Amongst these standards was *DITA.*

A modern definition of what we now mean by *structured authoring* is:

> A standardized methodological approach to the creation of content incorporating information types, systematic use of metadata, *XML*-based semantic mark-up, modular, topic-based information architecture, a constrained writing environment with software-enforced rules, content re-use, and the separation of content and form.

The separation of content and form

DITA has no native presentation format. Tagging within DITA simply labels what the information is, and not what it looks like. A phrase within a sentence may be a window name, and that is how it is marked up. This approach is known as *semantic mark-up*. Whether a semantically marked-up phrase eventually gets displayed in bold, or in red, or in a box, or not at all, is determined later, outside the authoring process.

Documents are never displayed to the reader in DITA; DITA is not a presentation format. *Content* is almost completely separated from *presentational form* and *delivery format.* Wherever possible, *context* is also separated from *content.*

In order to make editing friendlier, many DITA editing programs display the DITA content in a graphical user interface. This approach is described as *WYSIOO - What You See is One Option*. What you see as a DITA author may be nothing like how the reader will perceive the document, but it is one display option! (*WYSIOO* is a play on the familiar term *WYSIWYG*, or *What You See Is What You Get*.)

Where DITA fits...

Figure 46: DITA in relation to other standards and technologies

Diagram: *ComTech/Quadralay Presentation (Webinar), Jen Linton and Andrew VanConas*

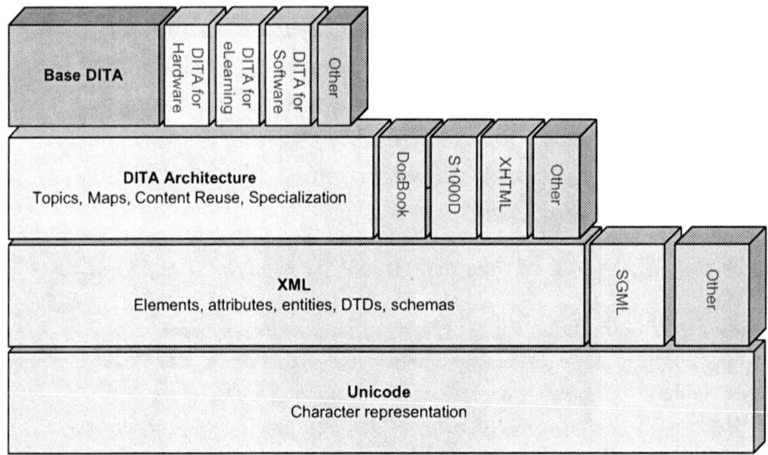

Inheritance

In object-oriented programming, inheritance is a way to form new program module *classes* using classes that have already been defined. DITA is designed around the principle of inheritance. The DITA base content model shows that even the three base information types (concept, task and reference) *evolve* from the `topic` *proto information type*, and share a common base structure whose characteristics they inherit.

Figure 47: Evolution of base information types

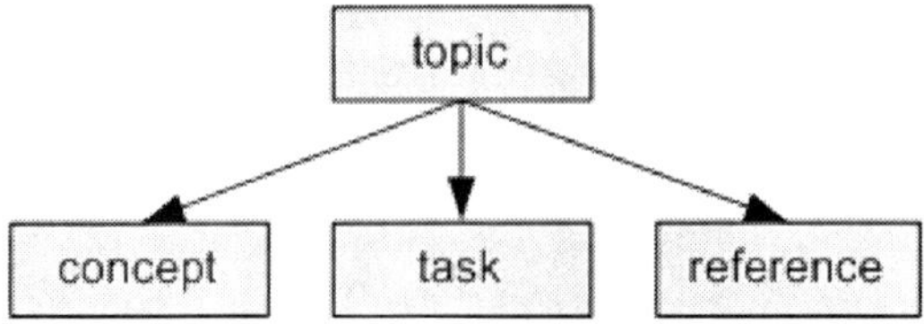

This idea of inheritance continues down. A task's `step` element is based on topic's `li` element.

The *DITA Language Reference* records the inheritance of each element. For example, the `step` element's inheritance is shown as `topic/li`, indicating that a `topic` information type's `li` element is specialized to become `task/step`, a `task` information type's `step` element.

DITA's inheritance model makes it easy to specialize topics or special elements within topics. You only have to define how the element is different from its immediate ancestor.

This idea reminds us again of Darwinian theory.

Figure 48: Evolution of man and an information type

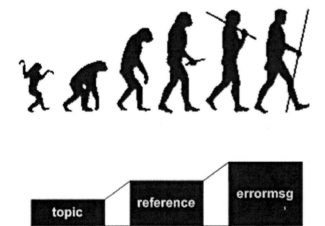

Conditions, filtering, variants and ditaval

Different technologies, and different authoring tools, use the terms *conditions, conditional publishing, variables, variants, flagging, profiling,* and *filtering* in different ways.

DITA has built-in features to enable some content to be excluded or highlighted during the publishing process. These features are standard metadata attributes that can be applied to most DITA elements, and a *ditaval* standard used to define how attributes are handled during publishing.

For example, the same topic might appear in an administrator manual and a consumer manual, but some paragraphs may only apply to the administrator. If those paragraphs are identified with an `audience` attribute of `administrator`, they can be conditionally excluded from the output if an `exclude` rule is defined in the *ditaval* file used for publishing.

In DITA, *conditional publishing* describes the process where the metadata and *ditaval* features are used together. Content identified with metadata attributes can be either *excluded* or *flagged* (highlighted in some way). Excluding content is commonly referred to as *filtering*.

The term *variable* is sometimes used within DITA authoring teams to describe a word, phrase or block of text that is managed in one place, usually through the content reference (*conref*) or key reference (*keyref*) feature. The term *variants* is not so commonly used, but may refer to two or more slightly different renditions of the same source topic.

Profiling is sometimes used to describe the technique of filtering the content displayed in a DITA editor based on the metadata attributes. (Not many DITA editors support profiling.)

Techniques to learn

DITA authoring requires you to have skills that you may have used in style-based authoring, but which you will certainly need to use differently. Some skills may be entirely new to you. These skills are:

Chunking
: Chunking refers to the way in which you break down information into smaller pieces. The term is particularly (but not exclusively) used to describe the way in which information is broadly categorized into *information types*, or *topic types*.

Labeling (or metadata creation)
: Labels and catalogue information are part of a topic's or collection's metadata. Metadata allows content to be filtered, sorted, processed, and otherwise manipulated. Choosing accurate labels will result in more flexible documents.

Linking
: Linking can be viewed as a technique for defining relationships between topics. In DITA, best practice is to link topics by defining the ways in which topics are

associated, rather than manually choosing what text is linked to which topic.

Separating content from form

In the writing phase of structured authoring, there is no place for *form* (format, style and presentation). Form is not the author's job. Content can be so separated by using semantics to identify each element of the document. For example, rather than think that a word needs to be displayed in bold, you need to think about what it is that makes it necessary to distinguish that word from the others.

Distinction between format and style, and data and metadata

The word "style" in "Style Guide" is problematic, because it has a number of subtly different meanings in this context. Style could mean aesthetic presentational style, and it could mean writing or wording style. A style could be clean and crisp (aesthetically) while being ponderous and wordy (stylistically).

To distinguish between the two "styles", *format* (or *presentational style*) should be used when referring to aesthetical style, or the look and feel of the deliverable document. The term *writing style* should be used when referring to the authorial style.

In the broader concept of the separation of content and form, *writing style* belongs to *content*, while *format* belongs to *form*.

The DITA Style Guide touches on writing style, but does not address format at all. It focuses on semantic mark-up, something that is not usually necessary in conventional style guides.

It is also important to understand the distinction between *data* and *metadata*. *Data* is analogous to *content*, while *metadata* refers to information **about** the content.

For example, the *data* of a topic is the information that the reader reads about the subject matter of the topic. The *metadata* is the supporting information about the topic that the reader doesn't normally read or see, such as the creation date, the author, the semantics of the textual components, and the copyright ownership. Metadata is usually more important to the author than it is to the reader.

Both *metadata* and *data* are in topics, but ditamaps should only contain *metadata*. (It is technically possible to store some data in ditamaps, but you should avoid this practice.)

Challenges for new DITA authors

In style-based authoring, the structure of a document is defined by the styles applied to its components. For example, a second level heading might be defined in a document by the application of a heading 2 style. Likewise, the presentational style of the deliverable document is defined by styles embedded within the authored document. For example, text to be indented by 2 cm might be defined in the paragraph by the application of an Indent2 style.

The separation of content and form in DITA sees the upper-level structure being defined outside the content (in the ditamap), and the presentational style being applied in a publishing process entirely separate from the authoring process. The presentational form for a document can be unknown to the DITA author. The same topic can have different appearances and different structures when the same source content is used to produce different deliverable documents.

For example, a DITA topic in one deliverable document may have a heading 2 style applied during processing, but the same topic in a different deliverable document may have heading 4 applied. The publishing rules determine the mapping of DITA semantic elements to output presentational form.

These differences between style-based authoring and semantic authoring present the greatest challenge to new DITA authors.

The blurred line between content and form

The difference between content and form is sometimes surprisingly difficult to identify.

For example, in the following sample, the word “Note:” looks like part of the content, but on deeper reflection, it turns out to be part of the presentational form.

The child restraint is now installed.

Note: Before having a child sit in the c
more firmly secured by pushing it dow

Parent topic: Safety

This becomes more obvious when you look at alternative ways of presenting the same information, such as the following:

The child restraint is now installed.

Tip

Before having a child sit in th
into the seat cushion and the

Parent topic: Safety

The child restraint is now installed.

Before having a child sit in the child re
secured. Sometimes a child restraint c
tightening the seatbelt.

Parent topic: Safety

The mark-up of that element in DITA must always follow the pattern:

```
<note>Before having...</note>
```

and never:

```
<note>Note: Before having...</note>
```

Embedding the label for an element in its text will limit the ways in which the element can be presented.

Ensuring that form is not mixed with content can be quite challenging when publishing tools don't make a sufficient distinction between text with a specific purpose and more general text. For example, when task topics are published through the default DITA Open Toolkit, no special formatting or labeling is applied to pre-requisite (`prereq`) elements. Avoid the temptation to add form to the content, and instead work to modify the publishing templates, stylesheets and processes so that the required formatting is applied during processing.

Ensuring that labels are applied in the publishing process rather than in the content will also simplify localization, as there is less text to translate.

Specialization

Although specialization is a key part of DITA, it is not yet a widely used feature. It is often viewed as being complicated and technical. But while specialization is often not used when it should be, the reverse is also true: specialization is sometimes used needlessly by organizations.

Specialization means defining your own information types and semantic elements and attributes to suit the needs of your particular content model (the nature of the type of information). A specialized element is always based on another DITA element, so that you only need to define how your element is different from what it is based on.

This specialization can only occur within DITA's specialization rules. In other words, it is a formal, defined process with specific rules. A specialization is defined by DTD or XSD modules that extend the base DITA DTDs and XSDs.

Organizations choose to specialize DITA because they want their documents to follow an organization-specific structure, or they want their documents to contain their own organization-specific metadata.

An example of a specialization to reflect a particular structure (or *content model*) is where you need a variation of a reference topic that contains part numbers, weight, wholesale price, and retail price. The base reference topic has a different structure, so you could specialize it with element names of `part_no`, `unit_weight`, `wsale_price`, and `retail_price`.

An example of a specialization to contain metadata is where you want to store the staff number of the programmer responsible for the software module being documented within the topic, in an attribute named `staff_number`.

Any specialized element or attribute has to be specialized from another DITA element. This element becomes the specialized element's *ancestor*.

When you publish a specialized topic, and the processor is not aware of your specialized information type, it will treat the topic as it would its ancestor.

If you need to exchange topics with someone who doesn't use your specialization, you might have to generalize the topics to return them to the structure of their ancestors. Generalization can be wholly automated.

Specialization rules in DITA include the following:

- You cannot make your specialized DITA less restrictive (have looser rules) than the DITA *base content model.*
  - You cannot make a mandatory ancestor element optional, and you cannot make a mandatory attribute optional.
  - You cannot allow elements in positions that are not allowed by the *base content model.*
- You cannot add new element-specific attributes. You can only create new global attributes (or attributes of elements in the *base content model.*

The DITA Style Guide focuses on base DITA.

Generalization

The opposite of specialization is *generalization.*

When topics are interchanged between authors or organizations, there may be a need to move content in specialized information types back to standard, base DITA information types. Likewise, when a document containing specialized information types is being processed to a delivery format through a publishing tool that is unaware of the specialization, the content must be transformed to a non-specialized, general DITA structure.

When processing a specialized element that it is not aware of, a processor (that is *specialization-aware*) will treat the element as though it is the *ancestor* element from which it "evolved".

For example, let's assume we have a specialized element called `part_desc` (based on the `propdesc` element) in a `parts_list` topic (based on the `reference` topic). When we transform that topic to HTML using a publishing tool, the processor, unaware of both `parts_list` and `part_desc` will just handle those elements as though they are `reference` and `propdesc` respectively.

Constraints

DITA 1.2 introduced the *constraints* feature.

A constraint defines a set of restrictions that conform to the rules of specialization. (The constraints mechanism was originally proposed as *replacement domains.*) Constraints aim to provide a more simplified authoring environment by restricting the mark-up options available to DITA authors to conform to business rules.

A constraint can remove an optional element from a content model, make an otherwise optional element required, and modify the attributes of an element by adding attributes or making them required. However, a constraint cannot make a mandatory element optional, and nor can it make a mandatory element optional.

Constraints are similar in purpose to specializations, but attempt to avoid the perceived technical complexity of specialization. They also allow non-semantic structural changes to be made without the specialization mechanism, which was designed more for semantic changes.

A constrained topic will always be valid as an unconstrained topic, as constraints only restrict what it permitted, not extend what is permitted. For example, if a constrained concept content model prevented `section` elements in a `concept` topic, a constrained concept topic would still be a valid concept topic, because the base content model allows a concept topic without a `section`.

The *strict task* information type in DITA 1.2 is actually a constrained *general task* information type.

Index

-dita-use-conref-target attribute value 175, 176

A

abbreviated-form element 39
abstract 78, 81
accessibility 151
acronyms 39
action 24, 98
action attribute 195
adoption
  levels of DITA 172
aesthetical style 229
agnostic
  presentation 125
align attribute 109, 144
alt attribute 151
alternative short description 83
alternative text 151
ampersand character 52, 156
ancestor 233
animation 147
apiname element 112
applets 147
architecture
  framework 11
  modular 223
  topic-based 223
area element 149
arguments 113
ASCII 122
assembly 223
attributes
  -dita-use-conref-target value 175, 176
  action 195
  align 109, 144
  alt 151
  audience 189, 190, 197
  char 109
  charoff 109
  chunk 19, 56
  class 69
  collection-type 40, 43, 45, 103
  colsep 109
  colwidth 109
  conaction 186
  conditional processing 189, 191
  conkeyref 143, 186
  conref 142, 163, 172, 177–179, 185, 186
  conrefend 185
  copy-to 54
  date 198
  expiry 198
  format 57, 157
  frame 109
  golive 198
  height 144
  href 52, 153, 156, 158, 199, 203
  id 67
  importance 99, 102, 166, 202
  keycol 106, 110, 111
  keyref 39, 143, 158, 159, 179
  keys 158, 159, 186
  linking 38, 40, 43, 49, 167, 181
  locktitle 57
  modified 198
  multiple values 191
  navtitle 42, 57
  otherprops 189, 190, 192, 197
  outputclass 69, 71, 201
  pgwide 109
  placement 144
  platform 189, 190
  print 32, 181, 197
  product 189, 190, 197
  props 192
  refcols 110
  restricting choice of values 191
  rev 189, 190
  rowheader 111
  rowsep attribute 109
  scale 109
  scope 40, 42, 57, 157, 158
  status 202
  toc 38, 181
  type 40, 42, 160, 161, 199
  valign 109
  width 144
  xml:lang 122
audience attribute 189, 190, 197
author comments 215
author element 199
authorial style 229
automatic linking 40, 49
automatically-generated links 31, 45

B

back matter
  page numbering 216
backslash character 52, 156
base content model 11, 13, 226, 232
best practice 8
block elements 64
BMP 141
body elements 65
bodydiv element 24
book 30
bookmap
  sample code 60
bookmap element 59
BookMaster 220
bookmeta element 59
booktitle element 59
brand element 199
breadcrumbs 49
broken link 58
bullet lists 84, 128
buttons 90

C

callouts 145, 147
capitals 130
Caroll, John 224
cascades
  in ditamaps 50
cascading style sheets 167
case 130
case-sensitive
  file and folder names 212
categories of elements 63
category names 120
cautions within steps 104
char attribute 109
character escapes 122
charoff attribute 109
chdesc element 106
chdeschd 106
chhead element 106
choice element 91
choice list 91
choices element 91
choicetable element 106, 110
choption element 106
choptionhd element 106
chrow element 106
chunk attribute 19, 56
chunking 20, 56, 228
class attribute
  HTML 201
cmd element 98, 102
cmdname element 112
CMS 198, 217
codeblock element 96, 119
codeph element 96
coderef element 119
cohesion 125
collection 30
collection-type attribute
  examples 47
colsep attribute 109
colspec element 109
colwidth attribute 109
command 98
command syntax 120
comments 68, 215
company names 120
complex tables 111
complex tasks 103
component element 199
composite information type 16
composite topics 16, 19, 20, 56, 184, 197
computer keyboard 118
conaction attribute 186
concept information type 13
concept topic
  title 132
condition attributes
  limiting 196
conditional processing
  cross-references 168
  dangers 193
  excluding topics 192
  in composite (ditabase) topics 197
  limiting 196
conditional publishing
  See conditional processing
conkeyref attribute 143, 186
connected blocks 91
conref
  -dita-use-conref-target value 176
  indexes 208
  organizing 182
  push 91, 186

spanning 24
See also conref attribute
conref attribute 67, 142, 163, 175, 177–179, 185, 186
conrefend attribute 185
constraints 83, 175, 210, 234
content assembly 223
Content Management System 217
See also CMS
content model 11, 13, 17, 26, 232
content re-use
conref push 186
finding elements to re-use 183
guidelines 174
indexes 208
organizing 182
referencing a conref transclusion 163
content reference
variables 179
See also conref
context 24, 127
context element 127
context-agnostic writing 173, 174, 196
controlled values 191
controlling element choices 210
conventions
attributes 192
file and folder names 212
formatting 120
coords element 149
copy-to attribute 54
copyrholder element 199
copyright element 199
copyryear element 199
created element 198
critdates element 198
critical dates 198
cross-references
in short descriptions 82
in title 169
indirect 159
related links 163
to a conref transclusion 163
to ditamap 167
to figures 160
to page number 161
to steps 162
to tables 161
to topics 155
CSS 71, 167, 201

D

dangling topicref 58
Darwin, Charles 219
Darwinian Theory 219
data element 72
data vs metadata 229
data-about element 72
date attribute 198
date format 198
dates 123
Day, Don 220
dd element 90
default topic 36
definition
content re-use 171
definition lists 84, 86, 90
definitions 86
delim element 120
delimiting attribute values 191
deliverable document 30
department names 120
dependent block elements 91
desc element 166
dialects 135
dialog 96
directory names 211, 212
disambiguation 23
DITA
authoring environment 225
definition 219
elements 63
features 222
framework 226
history 220
specialization 226
dita information type 16
DITA Maturity Model 172
DITA Technical Committee 27, 222
ditabase 16, 19, 20, 56, 184, 197
ditabase information type 16
See also ditabase
ditamap
bookmap 59
embedded 43
generated links 43, 44
hierarchy 43, 44

- linking to 167
- nested 43, 51
- separate reltable ditamap 43
- storing controlled values 191

ditamap elements 53
ditaval 179, 189, 195, 227
div elements 24
dl element 90, 145
dlentry element 90
DocBook 226
Document Development Life Cycle 198, 202
documentation process
- working in a team 210

domain elements 66
domain specialization 26
domains
- image map 75
- indexing 76
- metadata 76
- programming 73
- software 75
- typographic 78
- user interface 74
- utilities 75
- xNAL 76

draft-comment element 68, 215
dt element 90
DTD 73, 232
Dublin Core Metadata 203
duplicate semantic element names 69
duplicate topics 54
dynamically-merged Help 54

E

e-mail addresses
- linking to 157

Eberlein, Kris 80
Eclipse Help 36, 49
element domains 63, 73
element naming 214
elements
- abbreviated-form 39
- apiname 112
- area 149
- author 199
- body 65
- bodydiv 24
- bookmap 59
- bookmeta 59
- booktitle 59
- brand 199
- chdesc 106
- chdeschd 106
- chhead 106
- choice 91
- choices 91, 97
- choicetable 97, 106, 110
- choption 106
- choptionhd 106
- chrow 106
- cmd 102
- cmdname 112
- codeblock 91, 96, 148
- codeph 96
- coderef 119
- colspec 109
- component 199
- context 97, 127
- coords 149
- copyrholder 199
- copyright 199
- copyryear 199
- created 198
- critdates 198
- data 72
- data-about 72
- dd 90
- delim 120
- desc 166
- dl 84, 86, 90, 95, 145, 148
- dlentry 90
- domain 66
- draft-comment 68, 215
- dt 90
- entry 109
- featnum 199
- fig 68, 139, 142, 145, 148, 160
- fn 118
- glossref 39, 153, 156, 158
- image 105, 139, 141, 142, 144, 149
- imagemap 149
- index-see 206
- index-see-also 206
- indexterm 203, 205, 208
- info 102, 104, 105
- keydef 159, 179

keyword 69, 120, 179
keywords 199
kwd 69, 120
li 95
lines 96
link 52, 153, 156, 164, 166
linkinfo 166
linklist 164, 166
linkpool 164
linktext 42, 54, 164
lq 52, 91, 135, 136, 148, 153, 156
map 65, 167, 196
mapref 51, 196
metadata 199
msgblock 115, 148
msgnum 115
msgph 115
navref 54
note 94, 104, 230
object 147
ol 84, 95
oper 120
option 120
p 93–95
parml 90, 113
parmname 113
pd 90
ph 82, 119, 122, 178
platform 199
plentry 90
postreq 97, 127
  prereq
    link 99
    related-links 99
prodinfo 199
prodname 199
prognum 199
programming 73
prolog 65, 199
properties 110
pt 90
publisher 199
q 135, 136
refsyn 95
related-links 155, 163, 164, 167
relcell 30, 40, 49
relcolspec 40
relheader 30
relrow 30
reltable 30, 40, 167
required-cleanup 68, 215
result 127
revised 198
row 109
section 20, 68, 95
sectiondiv 24
sep 120
series 199
shape 149
shortdesc 78–80, 82, 83
simpletable 91, 93, 108, 110, 111, 148
sl 84, 91, 95
software 75, 76
source 52, 153, 156, 203
specialization 66
step 102, 104, 153, 162
stepresult 102
steps 97, 101
steps-informal 108
steps-unordered 108
stepxmp 105
subjectScheme 191
substep 101, 102
substeps 97, 101
synblk 120
synph 120, 122
system output 115
systemoutput 116
table 68, 86, 93, 108, 109, 111, 161
term 39, 158
text 119
title 40, 68, 129, 131, 132, 134, 145, 169
tm 117, 178
tophchead 30
topic 64, 68
topicgroup 30, 50
topichead 33, 53
topicmeta 30, 54, 83, 199
topicref 36, 38–40, 42, 49, 51, 52, 56, 57, 167, 192, 196, 197
typographic 78
uicontrol 118
ul 84, 95
user interface 75
userinput 118

utilities 76
var 69, 113, 120
varname 69, 113
vrmlist 199
xref 52, 149, 153–158, 160–163, 167–169
embedded ditamaps 43, 51
embedded links 24
embedded topics 184
English
varieties of 135
Enter key 118
entities 122, 180
entry element 109
enumerated attribute values 176
enumerated list
See controlled values
enumeration 89
EPS 141
escape characters 119, 122
evolution 219
examples
generated relationship links 31
excluding
content 195, 227
topics 192
exemplar
chunking attribute 73
conref 52, 156, 234
context-agnostic 52, 156
definition lists, APIs, commands, parameters, commands and codeblock 113
footnote 33, 172
inline cross-reference 27, 213
stub topic 21
tip 169
use of bold to stress words 192
use of lines element 205, 206
expiry attribute 198
extensions
file 213
external
cross-references 157

F

featnum element 199
fig element 68, 139, 142, 145, 148, 160
figure
titles 145
figures 68, 139, 148
file extensions 213
file formats
image 141
file management
conref referenced elements 181
image 142
file naming
conventions 211, 212
special characters 213
file structure
one topic per file 19
filtering
composite (ditabase) topics 197
conditional processing 192
ditamaps 196
finding re-use elements 183
flagging
during publishing 195
Flash 147
fn element 118
folder names 211, 212
folder structure 211
footnotes 118
foreign words and phrases 122
format attribute 157
format vs style 229
formatting conventions
syntax 120
frame attribute 109
front matter
page numbering 216

G

general task information type 14, 108, 234
generalization 232, 233
generated links
examples 47
GIF 141
glossary entry information type 15
glossary of terms 15, 158
glossentry information type 15
glossref element 39, 153, 158
glue text 125, 127
golive attribute 198
granularity 19, 98
graphics
different resolutions 143

group of elements
  transcluding a 185
GUID 67

H

hacks 68, 82
headings
  for related topic links 42
  levels 36
  styles 36
height attribute 144
Help systems 32
Hennum, Erik 220
hexadecimal character references 122
hierarchical links 43, 44
hierarchy 20, 29, 30
highlighting domain
  See typographical domain
history of DITA 220
home topic 36
Horn, Robert 224
hotspot graphics 149
hover text 79
href attribute 52, 153, 156, 158, 199, 203
HTML
  class attribute 201
  linking to 157
  map element 149
Hughes, Mike 21
human languages 135
Hunt, John 220
hypergraphics 76, 149
hyperlinks
  hiding in output 167
  related-links section 163
hyphenation 122

I

id attribute 67
ID Doc 220
identifying information types 17
IETF 213
IETF BCP 47 122
illustrations 139
image element 105, 139, 141, 142, 144, 149, 151
image file management 142
image maps 76, 149
imagemap element 149
images
  callouts 145
  within steps 105
  within title 145
importance attribute
  pre-requisite tasks 99
in-line links 155
in-text links 155
index-see element 206
index-see-also element 206
indexes
  multi-level 205
  secondary 205
  tertiary 205
indexing 203
indexterm element 203, 208
indirection 39, 159, 179, 186
info element 102, 104, 105
information architecture 221
Information Mapping 224
information types
  composite 16
  concept 13
  dita 16
  ditabase 16
  general task 14
  glossentry 15
  identifying 17
  reference 14
  specialized 26, 232
  task 13
  topic 16
inheritance
  in ditamaps 50
inline elements 64
inline images 139
intellectual property 117
Internet
  linking to 157
inverted commas 135, 136
ISO 639 122

J

Java applets 147

K

keyboard 118
keycol attribute 106, 110, 111
keydef element 159, 179
keyref attribute 39, 143, 158, 159
keys
  linking with 159
keys and labels 145
keys attribute 158, 159, 186
keystrokes 118
keyword element 69, 120, 179
keywords element 199
kwd element 69, 120

L

labeling 127, 131, 132, 228
labels
  for related topic links 42
  on images 145
language tags 122
languages
  content in different 135
lead-in sentences 87, 91
leader lines 145
legends 145
length
  topic 19
letter case 130
levels of DITA adoption 172
life cycle 202
limiting element choices 210
line breaks 96, 98, 131
lines 96
link element 99, 153, 164
link preview 79
linkinfo element 166
linking
  in tables 110
  indirect 159
  related-links section 163
  to ditamap 167
    See also links
linking attribute 40, 181
linking protocol 52, 156
linking relationships 40, 43
linklist element 164
linkpool element 164
links
  broken 58
  embedded 24
  generated 24, 45
  generated from ditamap 43, 44
  hiding in output 167
  in topics 155
  to Internet resources 57
  to PDF and other files 57
    See also linking
linktext
  specified in ditamap 83
linktext element 42, 54
list elements 95
list items 95
lists
  choice list in task topic 91
  definition list 90
  numbering style 89
  parameter list 90
  punctuation 128
localization
  graphics 147
localizing graphics 147
look-and-feel 71
lq element 135, 136, 153

M

management of content 217
managing DITA content 217
mandatory elements 83
mandatory steps 102
manifest 29, 32
map 32
map element 36, 167, 196
map element in HTML 149
map elements 65
map file
  sample code 60
map headings 53
map structure 60
mapref element 51, 196
maps
  nested 60
mark-up domains 73
mark-up languages
  marking up 96
master-slave Help systems 54
merge Help 54

messages
  system 115
metadata
  managing 198
  map level 29
metadata attributes
  conventions 192
  limiting 196
  multiple values 191
metadata domain 76
metadata element 199
metadata elements 199
metadata vs data 229
minimalism 125, 224
mixed content 93, 95
modified attribute 198
modular
  ditamaps 51
  documents 223
modular Help 54
mother-of-all-topics 33
movies 147
MPG 147
msgblock element 115
msgnum element 115
msgph element 115
multi-level indexes 205
multimedia 147
multiple navigation pathways 54
multiple values in attributes 191

N

names
  files 212
  files and folders 212
naming conventions 182, 214
navigation 29, 49
navref element 54
navtitle attribute 42
nested 87
nested block elements 91
nested content references 178
nested ditamaps 43, 51, 60
nested index entries 205
nested procedures 99
nested quotations 136
nested tables 111
non-breaking space 122
non-DITA content in ditamaps 57
non-sequential steps 108
note element 94, 104, 230
notes within steps 104
number type 89
numbered lists 84, 128
numbering
  page 216
numeric character references 122
Nurnberg Funnel 224

O

OASIS 27, 220, 222
object element 147
obsolete
  marking elements as 202
Ockham's Razor 81
On the Origin of the Species 219
onlytopic.in.map 58
open source 224
open standard 221
oper element 120
option element 120
optional steps 102
ordered lists
  numbering style 89
organization of elements 63
organizing re-use 182
otherprops attribute 189, 190, 192, 197
output 30
output styling 71
outputclass attribute 69, 71, 201
overriding topic metadata in the ditamap 83

P

page number references 161
page numbering 216
page references 153
pagination 216
paragraphs
  containing lists 87
  in reference topics 95
  inside notes 94
  within lists 95
  within table cells 93
parameter lists 90
parameters 113

parent topics 21, 23
parent-child links 43–45
parent-child relationships 38
parml element 90, 113
parmname element 113
pd entry 90
PDF
  linking to 157
peer 157
pgwide attribute 109
ph element 82, 122, 178
ph versus text 119
photo credits 139
phrase elements 64
phrase mark-up in titles 129
picking list 32
placement attribute 144
platform attribute 189, 190
platform element 199
plentry element 90
PNG 141
poetry 96
postreq element 127
pre-formatting text 96
pre-requisites 99
prereq element 99, 127, 166
presentational style 229
preventing automatic linking 49
preview text 79
previews
  topic 45
Priestley, Michael 172, 220
print attribute 32, 181, 197
print only content 193
print vs non-print 197
printouts 116
priority 202
procedures
  one per task topic 99
processes 24, 103, 108
processing
  conditional 189
processing output 30
processors 215
prodinfo element 199
prodname element 199
product attribute 189, 190, 197
product names 120
profiling 227
prognum element 199
program names 112
programming code 96
programming domain 73
programming domain elements 66
project names 120
project planning 202
prolog element 199
prolog elements 65, 198
properties element 110
props attribute 192
proto information type 16
protocol 52, 156
pt entry 90
publication 30
publisher element 199
publishing
  conditional 189
  process 215
  tools 215
punctuation
  lists 128
push 186

Q

q element 135, 136
QuickTime 147
quotation marks 135, 136
quotations 135, 136

R

re-use
  conref push 186
  finding elements to re-use 183
  guidelines 174
  organizing 182
read-outs from systems 116
reducing element choices 210
redundant elements 69
refcols attribute 110
reference information type 14
reference topic
  paragraphs in 95
  title 132
referenced element 175
referenced elements 181

references
  to page numbers 161
  to steps 162
referencing element 175
registered trademark 117
related topic links
  headings 42
related topics 164
related-links element 99, 155, 163, 164
related-links elements
  desc 166
  linkinfo 166
relationship links 31
relationship table
  hiding links 167
  links in 155
  linktext 42
  navtitle 42
relcell element 30, 40, 49
relcolspec element 40, 49
relheader element 30
relrow element 30
reltable
  examples of links 47
  headings for generated links 42
  hiding links 167
    See also relationship table
rendering engines 215
replacement domains 234
required-cleanup element 68, 215
resources
  links 52, 156
restricting available elements 210
result element 127
rev attribute 189, 190
review comments 215
revised element 198
Rockley, Manning, et al 221
role of a style guide 8
row element 109
row headings 110
rowheader attribute 111
rowsep attribute 109

S

S1000D 226
sample bookmap 60
sample code 96
scale attribute 109
scaling images 144
Scent of Information 79
Schell, Dave 220
schema 73
scope attribute 40, 42, 157, 158
secondary index entries 205
section element 68
section vs topic 18, 20
sectiondiv element 24
sections
  within topics 20
segmented hypergraphics 149
select attributes
  limiting 196
  multiple values 191
semantic mark-up 225
semantics 97
sep element 120
separation of content and form 20, 24, 109, 125, 131, 211, 224, 225, 228–230
sequence 20
serial commas 128
series element 199
service mark 117
set of elements
  transcluding a 185
SGML 220, 224, 226
shape element 149
short description
  specified in ditamap 83
shortdesc 81, 83
shortdesc element 78–80, 82
simple lists 84, 128
simple tables 111
simpletable element 108, 110, 111, 148
single sourcing
  graphics 143
single step procedure 101
size
  topic 19
skills 27
slash character 52, 156
SMB 52, 156
snippets 171, 182
software domain 75, 76
software domain elements 66, 75
source element 153, 203
span
  conref 185

special characters
in file names 213
special formatting of elements 230
specialization
domain 26
pros and cons 27
rules of 28
structural 26
types of 26
specialization elements 66
Spool, Jared 155
stages of the documentation process 209
standard
file and folder names 212
status attribute 202
STC 220
stem sentences 87, 91, 125, 127
stem topic 21
step element
cross-referencing 162
step references 162
stepresult element 102
steps
numbering style 89
steps element 97, 101
steps-informal element 108
steps-unordered element 108
stepxmp element 105
STOP 224
strict task information type 234
structural specialization 26
structure
separation of content and 20
structure of files and folders 211
structured authoring
definition 224
structured writing 224
stub content 125
stub topic 21, 33
style vs format 229, 230
styles
heading 36
subjectScheme element 191
submaps 43
subordinate block elements 91
subordinate topic preview 79
subordinate topics 21
substep element 101, 102
substeps element 99, 101
summary topics 33
SVG 139, 141, 147
SWF 147
Swope, Amber 172
symbols
in file names 213
synblk element 120
synph element 120, 122
syntax
formatting conventions 120
system messages 115
systemoutput element 115, 116

T

Tab key 118
table cells 93
table domain elements 66
table element 68, 108, 109, 111, 161
table entries 93
Table of Contents 32
tables
keycol attribute 110
nested 111
refcols attribute 110
types of 108
tabular information 109
tag abuse 68
task 24
task information type
syntax 97
task topic
syntax 97
title 132
team 210
term element 39, 158
terms 86
text element 119
text fragments 96
text versus ph 119
TIF 141
title element
images within 145
titles 68, 129
tm element 117, 178
TOC
excluding topics from 38
toc attribute 181
tool tips 79
top node in TOC 36

topic
  chunking 20
  length 19
  title 131, 132
topic element 68
topic elements 64
topic headings 53
topic hierarchy
  heading styles 36
topic information type 16
topic previews 45
topic references
  to non-DITA resources 57
topic structure 11
topic title 169
topic types
  identifying 17
topic vs section 18
topic-based authoring 32, 223
topical information unit 223
topical unit of discourse 223
topicgroup element 30, 50
topichead element 30, 33, 53
topicmeta 42, 83, 198
topicmeta element 30, 54, 199
topicref element
  attributes 45
trademark 117
transclusion
  -dita-use-conref-target value 176
  conref push 186
  of indexes 208
  organizing 182
  variables 179
transitional information 125, 127
translation
  graphics 147
type attribute 40, 42, 160, 161, 199
typographic domain 78
typographical domain elements
  in short descriptions 82

U

underscores in file names 212
Unicode 122, 226
unique identifiers 67
unit of discourse 18
unit testing 210
unordered lists
  bullet style 89
upper case 130
URI 52, 156, 213
URL 52, 156, 213
user input 118
user interface controls 90
user interface domain 74, 75
user interface domain elements 66
user interface messages 115
utilities domain 75, 76
utilties domain elements 66

V

validation 175
valign attribute 109
var element 69, 113, 120
variables 113, 171, 179, 182, 194, 227
variants 227
varieties 135
varname element 69, 113
video clips 147
vrmlist element 199

W

WAI 151
warnings within steps 104
Web
  linking to 157
Web only content 193
Web vs print 197
width attribute 144
windows
  open link targets in new 158
work instruction 24
workarounds
  conref 177
workflow 225
writing
  for re-use 173, 174
  paragraphs 134
writing style 229

X

XHTML 226
xml
  lang attribute 122
XML 220, 224, 226

XML comment 68, 215
XML languages
  documenting 122
xref element
  in shortdesc 82
XSD 73, 232
XSL-FO 215
XSL-T 215

LaVergne, TN USA
13 March 2011
219930LV00002B/5/P